Praise for *Prayers for a Heart-Shaped Life*

. . . .

"Karen Moore has done it again! She has an amazing way of clearing the fog of life and speaking right to my heart. Her latest book confirms that when our heart engages in prayer, big things happen. *Prayers for a Heart-Shaped Life* will help you discover even more of what God has in mind for you and the people you love. Give yourself a chance to go through each day prayerfully and heart-first."
                                        -Dr. Susan Sharpe, President, Intentional Living

"No matter how many books you've read on prayer, this new book by Karen Moore offers a unique perspective. . . A few moments of this book each day will soften and enrich your prayerful heart."
                                        -Dr. David L. Goetsch, Christian Counselor,
                                        Professor, and Management Consultant

"With *Prayers for a Heart-Shaped Life*, Karen reminds us how to offer prayers from the depths of our hearts to God, for our deepest needs and for the concerns of others."
                                        -Tom Kapella, Consultant: Business Strategy,
                                        Development, Customer Engagement

"The glory of believing in Christ, our Father God, and the Holy Spirit is that you get a fresh start every single day. What Karen Moore offers in *Prayers for a Heart-Shaped Life* is a way to put prayer front and center as you begin your day so God can guide you with His enduring grace and offer a path to forgiveness and even redemption. Whether you are familiar with prayer or lost when you try to communicate with the Lord, this book will help strengthen your faith as you seek that "peace that passes all understanding." God's love abounds in the pages of *Prayers for a Heart-Shaped Life*, so kick off every day with this wonderful book that will become an indispensable tool in your walk with Him."
                                        -Cameron Kim Dawson, Producer of *Letters to God,
                                        To Write Love on Her Arms*

"If you seek a deeper walk with Christ, begin your day with *Prayers for a Heart-Shaped Life*. Author Karen Moore's deep love for Christ is evident in every heart-shaped prayer. Whether you need a spiritual jump-start, a reminder of God's heart for the world, or a desire to be more like Jesus, you will be changed from the inside out as you make these prayers your own. There is no better day to begin than now."
-Dr. Andrea Mullins, Author, *Intentional Living,*
Choosing to Live for God's Purposes

"*Prayers for a Heart-Shaped Life* will open your mind and heart each day as you consider all that God intends for you and your family. Give yourself a nugget from this book each morning, and you will be amazed at how applicable that prayer will be for the particular need you face that day. Our God, who sees the heart, will hear your every prayer."
-Duane Ward, CEO, Premiere Marketing, LLC

Prayers
for a
Heart-Shaped
Life

Inspiring Prayers for
Living Life
Heart First

KAREN MOORE

SHILOH RUN  PRESS
An Imprint of Barbour Publishing, Inc.

© 2017 Karen Moore

Print ISBN 978-1-68322-320-7

eBook Editions:
Adobe Digital Edition (.epub) 978-1-68322-541-6
Kindle and MobiPocket Edition (.prc) 978-1-68322-542-3

Scripture quotations marked NIV are taken from the HOLY BIBLE, NEW INTERNATIONAL VERSION®. NIV®. Copyright © 1973, 1978, 1984, 2011 by Biblica, Inc.™ Used by permission. All rights reserved worldwide.

Scripture quotations marked MSG are from *THE MESSAGE*. Copyright © by Eugene H. Peterson 1993, 1994, 1995, 1996, 2000, 2001, 2002. Used by permission of NavPress Publishing Group.

Scripture quotations marked NCV are taken from the New Century Version of the Bible, copyright © 2005 by Thomas Nelson, Inc. Used by permission. All rights reserved.

Scripture quotations marked NLT are taken from the *Holy Bible*. New Living Translation copyright© 1996, 2004, 2015 by Tyndale House Foundation. Used by permission of Tyndale House Publishers, Inc. Carol Stream, Illinois 60188. All rights reserved.

Scripture quotations marked NKJV are taken from the New King James Version®. Copyright © 1982 by Thomas Nelson, Inc. Used by permission. All rights reserved.

Published by Shiloh Run Press, an imprint of Barbour Publishing, Inc., P.O. Box 719, Uhrichsville, Ohio 44683, www.shilohrunpress.com

Our mission is to publish and distribute inspirational products offering exceptional value and biblical encouragement to the masses.

Member of the
Evangelical Christian
Publishers Association

Printed in China.

Dear Friends,

It's always a good day to have a little chat with God. After all, He knows you like no one else ever could. He wants the best possible things for your life, and He is there for you anytime you call His name. In fact, talking with you is one of His favorite things to do.

God talks to you in prayer so you can make Him a priority and serve Him with the biggest love you can possibly muster. He wants you to love others, even as much as you love yourself—perhaps even more than that. Love fills your heart with each breath and helps you see the world with His eyes.

You are a recipient of the fullness of God's goodness and love. He answers your prayers and promises to be with you and lighten your heart whenever you draw near to Him. As it says in James 4:8 (NKJV), "Draw near to God and He will draw near to you."

One of the greatest gifts we ever receive happens at that moment when we realize that when we strive to understand God with our minds, we'll run into roadblocks. However, when we seek God with the depths of the heart, then nothing gets in the way of our relationship with Him. Seek Him and you will find the One who made earth and heaven. Offer Him your prayers, and give Him praise and thanks as your spirit grows stronger, lavished by His love!

May God grant your heart's desires and hear your prayers with grace and mercy as you strive to live a more heart-shaped life.

With prayers of love,
Karen Moore

Your Prayers for a *Heart-Shaped Life—* Talk to God Every Day

. . . .

Tell God all that is in your heart,
as one unloads one's heart,
its pleasures and its pains,
to a dear friend.
Tell Him your troubles,
that He may comfort you;
tell Him your joys,
that He may sober them;
tell Him your longings,
that He may purify them;
tell Him your dislikes,
that He may help you conquer them;
talk to Him of your temptations,
that He may shield you from them:
show Him the wounds of your heart,
that He may heal them.

FRANÇOIS FENELON

As I Wait for the Lord

....

*O LORD, hear me as I pray; pay attention to my
groaning. Listen to my cry for help, my King and
my God, for I pray to no one but you. Listen to my
voice in the morning, LORD. Each morning I bring
my requests to you and wait expectantly.*

PSALM 5:1–3 NLT

Lord God,

Morning after morning, I come before You, seeking Your kindness and favor. No one else can turn my life around, granting me a renewed spirit and a heart filled with hope.

Help me today to wait patiently for Your answers to those things that weigh me down. My hope is in You, and so I lift up my heart to You in every circumstance I face, trusting and believing in Your strength and mercy.

Hear me, Lord, with ears that vibrate with grace; see me with eyes of tenderness.

I am grateful to You this very day.

Amen.

Shape My Thoughts

At that time Jesus said, "I praise you, Father,
Lord of heaven and earth, because you have hidden
these things from the people who are wise and smart.
But you have shown them to those who are like little
children. Yes, Father, this is what you really wanted."

MATTHEW 11:25–26 NCV

Dear Lord,

Sometimes I'm surprised by the unruly thoughts that come into my head, totally unbidden, totally odd because they are so out of character for me or the things I struggle to understand about the world. I ask You today to shape my thoughts, giving me a clean heart and a genuine love for the people closest and dearest to me.

I pray for a childlike faith, the kind that accepts and trusts and lives in Your protection and Your love. Wrap Your arms around my heart and mind, and help me to think only on those things that are from You.

Fill me with kind thoughts toward all others—thoughts that are worthy of You—so I'll act with a loving heart in all I do.

Amen.

Heart-Shaped Promises

For no matter how many promises God has made,
they are "Yes" in Christ. And so through him the
"Amen" is spoken by us to the glory of God.

2 CORINTHIANS 1:20 NIV

Father in heaven,

I'm eternally grateful for Your promises that sustain my life and provide for my needs each day. I thank You for my beautiful home and my loving family, and for my work and good health. My heart overflows with joy because You allow me to lean in and listen to Your voice anytime at all. Thank You for Your steadfast love and Your everlasting arms of strength whenever I feel weak. I rejoice that You anticipate my needs even before I realize what I may be missing and that You go before me wherever the day takes me.

Above all, Father, I thank You for being willing to shape my heart to be more like Jesus. I thank You for saying yes to the many prayers I've whispered and shouted and sung to You over the years. I cannot praise You enough for guiding my heart, my mind, and the work of my hands. I pray today that I will honor You in all I do.

Amen.

At the Heart of Grace

··

Let your conversation be always full of grace, seasoned with salt, so that you may know how to answer everyone.

Colossians 4:6 niv

Dear Lord,

Sometimes I know I'm too passive about my approach to You or the ways I share Your love with others. Lately, I realize that when I come to You in prayer or I speak of You when I'm in social circles, my efforts lack power; they lack the fervor I had when our relationship began. Forgive me when I stand on the edge of faith, standing near You but not embracing You. I'm ready to open up now and pour out my love for You wherever I am.

Season me with the salt of Your Holy Spirit. Help me to be more robust and certain when I speak of You or share time with You in prayer. Please fill me up so Your light comes through as part of every conversation I may have today. Sprinkle goodness from Your grace on the head and heart of each person I meet.

Let me be seasoned with the salt of Your love and share that salt generously with those around me. You are the salt of the world, and my heart thirsts for You today.

Amen.

Abide, Wait, Spend a Little Time with Me!

* *

*Wait on the LORD; be of good courage, and He shall
strengthen your heart; wait, I say, on the LORD!*
PSALM 27:14 NKJV

Dear Lord,

Sometimes my heart is at a loss, insecure in what it truly means to wait for You. I wonder if waiting means I should just do nothing and leave everything in Your hands. That could be right.

Or I question whether I should keep doing all I can while I wait, just in case my "help" is needed. Or maybe I could even go on ahead so I'm ready for when You arrive, and then we could get things done.

I look at all those options, though, and I realize none of them are right or all of them are right. My heart awakens to the idea that perhaps all You want from me is to simply be there, right beside You, trusting You. Maybe all You want is for me to wait with a believing heart.

I ask You to strengthen my heart today so I can be of good courage, believing in all You will do when the time is right. Help me to sit peacefully at Your side today, knowing You will work all things together for my good.

Amen.

The Heart of "Abba"

*Because you are his sons, God sent the Spirit of his Son
into our hearts, the Spirit who calls out, "Abba, Father."
So you are no longer a slave, but God's child; and since
you are his child, God has made you also an heir.*

GALATIANS 4:6–7 NIV

Dear Daddy,

Thank You for taking my hand and allowing me to be Your beloved child. You've called me by name, and You've created a new heart within me so that I might come to You in all joy and innocence and get to know You better. You've beckoned me to be in a relationship with You, and You've allowed me to seek Your face whenever I feel lost or afraid or uncertain about the turmoil of life.

Thank You for reminding me today that You are as close to me as any father can be, that You are my "daddy" in heaven, the one who sees me and loves me just as I am. You accept me because of Your Son, Jesus. You draw me close to You and let me listen to Your voice.

As Your child, I thank You for loving me so much and for keeping me close to You each day. Help me to be more like You, more like my Father, every day. I ask You this in the beautiful and powerful name of Jesus.

Amen.

The Talent Search

We have different gifts, according to the grace given to each of us. If your gift is prophesying, then prophesy in accordance with your faith; if it is serving, then serve; if it is teaching, then teach; if it is to encourage, then give encouragement; if it is giving, then give generously; if it is to lead, do it diligently; if it is to show mercy, do it cheerfully.

ROMANS 12:6–8 NIV

Lord,

It's clear that You did not give each of us the same kinds of abilities or talents. We are each uniquely designed. Some of us create amazing ideas, artwork, books; others dance across a stage and entertain appreciative audiences. The kinds of abilities You've given us are too numerous to even recount, but one thing makes sense to my heart.

In this vast, amazing world of millions of people, You know me. You know who I am and what I can do. You designed me perfectly for the role You wanted me to play when I came to earth.

Today, Lord, I ask You to search my heart, not simply to confirm my belief in You, but to remind me of my purpose, of the very reason You wanted me to develop talents I could use to help others. Bless the work of my hands and each one of us who seek Your direction for our lives. Help us to cheerfully lead, teach, bless, and encourage others according to Your will and Your good pleasure.

Amen.

Making an About-Turn

The kind of sorrow God wants makes people change
their hearts and lives. This leads to salvation,
and you cannot be sorry for that.

2 Corinthians 7:10 NCV

Father in heaven,

I made an about-turn some years ago when I first received You into my heart. It was a glorious day, and I often give thanks that You called me to be Your child.

Sometimes I still feel a need to make an about-turn for the little things in my life that may bring me sorrow, things I do that may displease You, or things that simply do not serve me well. Help me to become more of what You want me to be in my personal life, my prayer life, and my work life. I want to hand over the reins of my life to You and turn to You in all I do. I want to live a life that is heart-shaped and molded by Your love and grace and mercy.

I seek Your face today, Lord, knowing I will always need Your tender guidance to keep me walking in the right direction. I pray for others, too, who may need to turn again to You for the things that make life worthwhile and the things that keep them close to You. Thank You for giving me a softer, more pliable heart so I'm more open to sharing Your love with others.

Amen.

The Heart of Acceptance

And the Spirit and the bride say, "Come!" And let him
who hears say, "Come!" And let him who thirsts come.
Whoever desires, let him take the water of life freely.

REVELATION 22:17 NKJV

God of my heart,

I know that You offer me living water and the chance to be free in You. You have given me an open invitation, and it is my desire to always come to Your table.

Thank You for loving me so much that You provided living water, this refreshing and thirst-free way to come back to You. Thank You for knowing me even before I left my mother's womb and for believing in me enough to be sure I discovered Your love as I grew.

Today I pray for everyone I know to be drawn to You as the source of living water. I pray that You will draw near to my friends and family and those I love so they find acceptance and love in Your eyes. I pray that they will thirst in new ways to come to know You with their hearts and minds.

Thank You for Your immeasurable love and grace and mercy on us all. Thank You for inviting all of us into Your heart for all eternity.

Amen.

A Gravelly Heart

. . . .

*"I will give you a new heart and put a new spirit
within you; I will take the heart of stone out of
your flesh and give you a heart of flesh."*

 EZEKIEL 36:26 NKJV

Dear Father,

You have done marvelous things. You have blessed me with Your Spirit and caused me to grow in knowledge, awareness, and love of You and the people around me. You have made me whole.

Today I ask that You would help me with whatever parts of my heart are still resistant to Your touch. Help me to surrender all I am to You so I may have a heart of kindness and compassion and one that beats with love. Forgive those stony parts of my heart that may still have sway within me, the ones I continue to foster even when I know better. Give me a softer heart for those times when life is hard or things don't go my way.

I realize I have a lot to learn about what it means to have a tender heart, but I trust You to show me how to open doors to loving myself and others in ways I have not been able to do before. Give me, Lord, a tender heart and a peaceful soul.

Thank You for Your infinite love.

Amen.

At the Heart of the Matter

....

*Jesus answered and said to him, "Most assuredly, I say to you,
unless one is born again, he cannot see the kingdom of God."*

JOHN 3:3 NKJV

Father God,

Sometimes I think the human side of me is still blind, unable
to see very clearly all that You want from me and for me. I'm like a
toddler, falling and getting up again, learning to walk behind You
and follow You so I can grow strong. I pray for the eyes of my heart
to be opened in new ways, ways that have eluded me before, so
that I can walk in peace today. I pray to be born anew in ways that
help me see what I can do for the good of Your kingdom.

Uncover my eyes, Lord, so I can see that You are still in control
of all that happens here on earth and that You have great plans for
the people who love and serve You. Open my mind to hear Your
voice in my conversations with others and in the words I read in
scripture. Make me aware of You in all the things that I do.

I thank You for drawing me to the place where I could be born
again and for sharing the light of Your Spirit to live within me. Help
me to live each day so that I might be a living example of Your
grace and mercy and love.

Amen.

Wake Up!

Love never hurts a neighbor, so loving is obeying all the law.
Do this because we live in an important time. It is now time
for you to wake up from your sleep, because our salvation
is nearer now than when we first believed.

ROMANS 13:10–11 NCV

Eternal Father,

It is always my prayer to be more loving. Sometimes I think I do it well; but often, I realize that I fall far short of the mark. After all, I'm loving to the people who are in my inner circle, but I don't make much of an effort to be more loving to those I meet in various ways throughout the day.

Help me to be intentional about sharing my love for You so that it simply spills over in my conversations when I'm in the grocery store, or an office, or even walking down the street. Help me to reflect the light of Your love anyplace I happen to go today.

I know that I can be a bit sleepy, not really awake or aware of the needs of others who may be looking to me to get to know You better. Wake me up in every area of my life where I can make a difference and where I can show what it means to have the light of Christ within my soul.

Amen.

Success and Failure!

*Plans fail for lack of counsel,
but with many advisers they succeed.*
PROVERBS 15:22 NIV

Lord,

You know I'm a planner. I love to make lists and set up schedules and figure out exactly when I should do something to achieve a goal. However, I've learned that being a planner is only one part of the formula for success. The rest of it is determined by wise counsel and by keeping my heart aligned to Yours.

Today, I seek Your voice, Your counsel on any plans that I have in front of me. I ask You to guide me to the right people who would be Your choices to help me succeed in my goals. I ask You to bless the work of my hands in the projects I intend to do—the ones that occupy my lists of things to achieve. I ask that I would work within Your will in every way.

I know, Lord, that there is only one true success in this world, and that is to do the work You have called me to do, surrendering everything else to achieve Your will and purpose, for with You alone can my plans succeed. Thank You for Your counsel and the counsel of others You bring into my life today.

Amen.

Stretch My Faith

. . . .

*When Jesus looked out and saw that a large crowd had
arrived, he said to Philip, "Where can we buy bread to
feed these people?" He said this to stretch Philip's faith.
He already knew what he was going to do.*

JOHN 6:5–6 MSG

Creator God,

You are the only one who knows what needs to happen to
help us grow in faith. You alone create and mold and stretch us
to become more than we were before. You know who we are and
what we are. You understand us from the inside out. You make
Yourself clear to our hearts, and we are grateful.

Thank You for Your divine intervention, Your willingness to make
me more than I would ever be on my own. Thank You for taking
me out of my comfort zone so I am stretched further to produce
greater work for Your kingdom. Only You know how to stretch me
without breaking me. Only You know the work You have designed
for me to do. Help me to be flexible, able to bend and move and
strive to shine Your light in joy.

Thank You for holding me in the palm of Your hand! Thank You
for giving me new opportunities to serve You.

Amen.

A Heart-Shaped Question

. . . .

That night God appeared to Solomon and said to him, "Ask for whatever you want me to give you." Solomon answered God, "You have shown great kindness to David my father and have made me king in his place. Now, LORD God, let your promise to my father David be confirmed, for you have made me king over a people who are as numerous as the dust of the earth. Give me wisdom and knowledge, that I may lead this people, for who is able to govern this great people of yours?"

2 CHRONICLES 1:7–10 NIV

Dear Lord,

When I think of the question You posed to Solomon, I'm awed. I'm awed by Your question, and I'm awed by Solomon's response. It is no wonder that You honored him for simply asking to be wise so he could make good choices and worthy decisions to lead Your people.

I believe in my heart that You ask each of us that question. You come to us and suggest that we can ask You for whatever we need. If our need is for better health, a better financial position, more love, or greater ability to do our job or to raise our children with integrity, then it occurs to me that our answer should be the same as that of Solomon. Our answer should be to have Spirit-filled wisdom.

In my heart, I know that only with wisdom can I make the kind of choices that creates a difference. Only seeking Your face and Your voice in all I do can truly cause me to be the person You have raised me up to become.

Bless me and all Your children who seek Your guidance, and grant each of us wisdom today.

Amen.

Becoming More Holy

. . . .

He has saved us and called us to a holy life—
not because of anything we have done but
because of his own purpose and grace.

2 TIMOTHY 1:9 NIV

Dear Lord,

You have redeemed us so we can fulfill Your purposes. You have blessed us with gifts and talents and abilities to be used for Your service. You have covered us with grace and eternal love.

You have done all of that, yet it is still difficult to feel "holy." I pray today that You would help me understand more clearly what it truly means to be holy in Your presence or to act in ways that are holy while I'm living in this body here on earth. Help me to see what is "holy" even in the more mundane activities of the day—things like cleaning a house, driving a car, or doing the weekly shopping chores.

Help me to desire a holy heart, one that is wholly and wonderfully dedicated to You and one that is willing to step out and reach up to do all I can do to bless those You put in my care. Give me a holy heart, a loving heart, and a kind heart so I can represent You anywhere I go.

Amen.

Designed to Walk in Love

. . . .

*Follow God's example, therefore, as dearly loved children
and walk in the way of love, just as Christ loved us and gave
himself up for us as a fragrant offering and sacrifice to God.*

EPHESIANS 5:1–2 NIV

Dear Lord,

You gave me the gift of faith. Long ago You planted Your
Spirit within my heart and asked me to follow You. Ever since our
story began, I've been doing my best to keep up with You. I know
that sometimes I walk ahead of You, and then I lose my way or I
make bad choices. Other times I hang back and don't draw near
to You as much as I need to do so I can stay strong and stay on
the course You intended.

Help me today to walk in stride with You, walking in love and
in all the ways that bless those around me. Remind me of all we've
done together so far and what joy it brings my heart when I don't
try to handle life alone. Grant me more grace to keep my mind,
heart, and soul walking with You.

I ask, too, that You would give me the heart of a child, stubbornly
believing that You will always deliver on Your promises, living in
hope that nothing will keep You from me in dark hours, and trusting that I will always recognize the path You would have me take.

Amen.

Feed My Sheep

The third time he said to him, "Simon son of John, do you love me?" Peter was hurt because Jesus asked him the third time, "Do you love me?" He said, "Lord, you know all things; you know that I love you." Jesus said, "Feed my sheep."

JOHN 21:17 NIV

Father in heaven,

You know all things. You know that I love You and do my best to serve You. You know what makes me strong and keeps me close to You; and You know just as well the things that separate me from You and cause me to disappoint You and the relationship we share.

It is my desire to serve You and to help others come to know You in a personal way. I know that for a good shepherd to be able to feed a flock, the shepherd must be willing to lead and to give from the heart. I ask to be that kind of shepherd and, in ways that please You, to feed the flocks that are in my care.

You've called my name, and You've asked me to walk with You and be Your ambassador. Please help me to do my work with great love for You and with great respect for others so I can serve You well.

Help me to have the inspired heart of a shepherd as I do Your work in Jesus' name today!

Amen.

Doing the Right Thing

. . . .

*Remember, it is sin to know what
you ought to do and then not do it.*

JAMES 4:17 NLT

Dear Lord,

I have sinned against You. I know that many times I could have chosen to do the right thing, because I knew the right thing to do; but for some reason, I did the wrong thing anyway. It grieves my heart when I let my ego guide my actions or I allow my own stubborn opinions to be my guides. I can only imagine that it grieves Your heart, too, because every action comes with a consequence.

Thank You for Your steadfast love and Your willingness to forgive me when I yield to the temptation of putting money on a credit card that I already can't pay, or when I share something with someone else that wasn't mine to share. Forgive me when I don't take time to pray or when I don't reach out to help others in all the ways that I know You would have me do. Forgive not only those offenses I've so knowingly committed but also those that I committed blindly.

Help me be more willing to listen to Your voice so You can guide my heart in every way. Help me to do the right thing—the thing that always pleases You!

Amen.

Bless the Mean People

"But I say to you who are listening, love your enemies.
Do good to those who hate you, bless those who
curse you, pray for those who are cruel to you."
LUKE 6:27–28 NCV

Dear Lord,

I want so much to be a child of Your light, one who loves others unconditionally and lives a truly heart-shaped life. The problem is that loving some people is simply not easy. It's hard to find the good in what they do or say. It's hard to understand their cruelty to others and even to me.

Today I pray for all the people who do not truly understand what it means to love others, people who bring insult and injury to conversation, or people who abuse others because they live with an angry spirit. Lord, bless those people so they can turn toward You, toward Your light of love, and learn to be better people. Help me to be willing to bless them when they are unkind. Let me never offer unkind words in return. Even more, Lord, I pray that I will never be one of those mean people, even unintentionally.

Teach us all to love others as You love them and to lift them up to You for deliverance. Fill us with a spirit of kindness and compassion wherever we may be today. Thank You for protecting people everywhere from abuse and for watching over the hearts and minds of those who seek You in prayer.

Amen.

The Battle for Your Heart

. . . .

Try to do good, not evil, so that you will live, and the LORD
God All-Powerful will be with you just as you say he is.

AMOS 5:14 NCV

Father in heaven,

Some days I feel like I'm entering a battlefield as soon as I go outside my door. I seek Your face and listen for Your voice in the sanctuary of my home, but then the world assaults my ears and my eyes as soon as I step into it. I am saddened by the people I see who are so willing to be unkind to others and who are so blinded by ego they do not even know You are there.

I know that the earth is a battleground and that our hearts are the prize. Evil tries to establish itself in the hearts of all of us, and it does so in ways that are not always easy to recognize. It curls up like a snake at our doors and pulls at us when we're disappointed by life, causing us to question if You're still with us. It laughs at us when we struggle to pay our bills or to manage our health or try to understand our unruly children. It seems to be everywhere visible and invisible.

In this good-and-evil battle, we need Your protection. We need to draw near to You and feel Your presence. Help me and those I love to put on the full armor of God so that we can find security in Your embrace. I ask You these things in Jesus' name.

Amen.

Change: Adopt or Adapt

. . . .

"God is not a human being, and he will not lie. He is not a human, and he does not change his mind. What he says he will do, he does. What he promises, he makes come true."

NUMBERS 23:19 NCV

Dear God,

I know that You don't change. You are the same now as You were when You set the stars in the sky and put human beings on the earth. You brought all things together for the good of everyone. I fervently pray to be more like You so that I always deliver on my promises and do the things I say I will do. I pray that I might do what You have called me to do each day.

Sometimes my intentions are good, but nothing goes as planned. The car breaks down or the Internet stops working or the kids need extra help, and by the time I'm ready to get back to work, the day is spent. Those changing circumstances often alter my direction and my thinking.

Lord, help me remember that human beings often change their course, especially when we forget to seek Your counsel and direction before we act. Help me to give more grace to others when they change plans and expectations with me.

Grant that I would be steadfast in seeking You in all things, building on Your foundation of love for all of us, a love that is forever true.

Amen.

Adorable You!

. . . .

*"The Father himself loves you. He loves you because
you loved me and believed that I came from God."*

JOHN 16:27 NCV

Father in heaven,

I thank You today for what You've done in my life. You have
lifted me up and placed me on a pedestal simply because of Your
love for me. You have embraced me with Your whole heart and have
stood beside me since the day I first called Your name. You have
been my mentor and teacher, my healer and helper, my friend and
companion. There is no relationship on this earth more precious
to me than the one we share.

Today, I also pray for the people I know who do not yet realize
they can be adored by You. I pray that they would see Your hand at
work in their lives in ways that they cannot miss and be filled with
a desire to know You better. I pray this for friends and family and
coworkers and all who need to feel the warmth of Your embrace.

Help me to enthusiastically share what it means to be adored
by You. Help me to tell everyone I know of Your love.

Amen.

An Unhappy Heart

. . . .

*The Lord GOD has put his Spirit in me, because
the LORD has appointed me to tell the good news to
the poor. He has sent me to comfort those whose
hearts are broken, to tell the captives they are free,
and to tell the prisoners they are released.*

ISAIAH 61:1 NCV

Dear Lord,

This passage from Isaiah reminds me that I have, at some point in my life, been all of the people spoken about in this text. I have been in poverty, both poverty of spirit and of financial resources. I have been brokenhearted about events in my life or relationships that suffered beyond repair. Lord, I've even been imprisoned—not by some public jail, but from thoughts that hold me back and keep me from becoming all that You would have me be. Sometimes I've even been imprisoned by my own unwillingness to forgive others or to change direction.

Set me free, Lord. Set me free to worship You with my whole heart, to share my gifts and talents with the world, and to encourage others that they are indeed free because You have made them free.

Bless all those who feel stuck or who are blinded by their own choices and help them to see You more clearly today. Change their unhappy hearts to a place where they live life in total joy. Thank You, Lord.

Amen.

At the Heart of Grace

. . . .

And He said to me, "My grace is sufficient for you,
for My strength is made perfect in weakness."
2 CORINTHIANS 12:9 NKJV

Lord God,

I am grateful for the opportunity to walk in Your grace and mercy. The world is a slippery slope, and I am not always prepared for its twists and turns. Sometimes I'm not equipped to handle the sudden changes that leave me hanging from a cliff of despair, grasping for Your hand and gasping for air.

Sometimes I make the wrong choices or I take the wrong road and miss the good things You have set for me. When I do, I thank You for sending me a lifeline, extending Your grace to keep me close to You. When I am weak, You are especially strong, able to hold on to me and keep me from falling too far from Your side. Thank You for giving me room to grow and change, room to make mistakes and be forgiven, and room to love and learn and try again.

Lord, I pray for all those who feel weak, uncertain, or unprepared for whatever the day may bring, that they would feel You close beside them, guarding and guiding and giving them strength to do what must be done.

Thank You for blessing our lives with Your grace and Your powerful strength and love.

Amen.

Refreshing Your Heart and Mind

. . . .

And do not be conformed to this world, but be transformed
by the renewing of your mind, that you may prove what
is that good and acceptable and perfect will of God.

ROMANS 12:2 NKJV

Father in heaven,

It is the prayer of my heart to follow You and seek Your guidance as I move through the world. I ask that You would help me not be tempted by the distractions of the day, those things that waste my time and keep me from doing Your work. Help me to be on guard and speak in ways that please You. Keep me from being swayed by the ideas or opinions of a group I'm with socially, to the place that I forget who I am spiritually.

Renew my mind, granting me a spirit of love and a spirit of willingness to serve You according to Your purpose for my life. Help me to desire more of You and less of what the culture of the moment tries to persuade me to be. Help me in all circumstances to be willing to shine Your light.

I pray for those who place hope in You and strive for the transformation that truly comes from Your Spirit. Direct our hearts and minds toward Your perfect will.

Amen.

You're a Bit of Royalty

The Spirit Himself bears witness with our spirit that we
are children of God, and if children, then heirs—heirs
of God and joint heirs with Christ, if indeed we suffer
with Him, that we may also be glorified together.

ROMANS 8:16–17 NKJV

My heavenly King,

It's amazing to think that I am a child of a King, a direct descendant of the Creator of the world and an heir with Christ my Lord in Your kingdom. In fact, it's so amazing that most of the time I cannot truly fathom what it means. I know You have called my name and found me acceptable to be Your child because of my love for Jesus. I know that someday I will share a glorious home with You in heaven, and that is a beautiful thought indeed.

Today, my Lord, I pray for all the people who don't yet know You as their Lord and Savior. I pray for those who wander in the labyrinth of life and have no idea where they are going and what they are even doing here. I pray for those who have a deep desire to find connection and love and a sense of family and all the things they can discover if they draw close to You.

Be with each of us as we learn what it means to be a child of God. Help us to be worthy heirs bearing witness to Your love everywhere we go.

Amen.

A Child of Tomorrow

"I say this because I know what I am planning for you,"
says the LORD. "I have good plans for you, not plans
to hurt you. I will give you hope and a good future."
JEREMIAH 29:11 NCV

Dear Lord,

I'm struggling today. I can't seem to see the end of the path where things turn in a positive direction. My work seems to be going nowhere, my relationships are stretched to the limit because of my worries, and I wonder what the future will look like when the present is so very bleak.

For a long time now, I've tried to be a faithful child, looking for Your guidance, seeking for direction through scripture, and hoping that my prayers will be answered. I thank You for the many times You've heard me cry and lifted me up to a better place, reminding me of the reasons to smile.

I believe You and only You can direct my steps and lead me to a brighter future. I ask today that You would help me to feel Your presence in every place I might be. Embrace my heart, and grant me wisdom and strength, renewing my hope and sense of peace. I pray this for myself and for all who struggle with life today.

Amen.

A Wise Heart

I saw that being wise is certainly better than being foolish, just as light is better than darkness.

ECCLESIASTES 2:13 NCV

Dear Lord,

It may be an old-fashioned idea to pray for wisdom, but it feels like something that's far more important than anything else I might ask You to provide. After all, wisdom can change the direction of my thoughts, help to develop the work of my hands, and bring light to my heart and mind.

Thank You for Your willingness to guide me and Your patience to sustain me even when I behave in foolish ways. Thank You for coming back time and again to set me on the right path. Thank You for knowing me far better than I know myself.

Help me to be wise in the ways that cause my spirit to rejoice and my heart to be light. Show me what You would have me do with every step I take, and bless each conversation with Your divine love so that I am a voice of reason and kindness. More than anything, Lord, I pray to have a wise heart that follows You in all I do today.

Amen.

Believe with Your Whole Heart!

Then Jesus touched their eyes and said, "Because you believe I can make you see again, it will happen."

MATTHEW 9:29 NCV

Dear Lord,

You touch people's lives every hour of the day. You heal us from our blindness, our dark thoughts, and our foolishness. You watch over the things we do and help us when we lose our way.

I pray today, Lord, that You would help me to trust You for everything in my life. Help me believe for the financial stability that I seek. Help me believe for the right opportunities to serve You. Help me believe for the health and welfare of my body, my home, and my family. Grant me the faith to seek You in all things.

I pray, not only for myself, but for all people who look to You in hope, who pray to You each day, and who depend on You for their daily bread.

Forgive my unbelief. Remove the blind spots that exist in my eyes, and help me to see Your hand at work in my life today. Grant me a believing heart. Thank You, Lord, for Your kindness to me.

Amen.

A Long-Suffering Heart

*Blessed is the one who perseveres under trial because,
having stood the test, that person will receive the crown
of life that the Lord has promised to those who love him.*

JAMES 1:12 NIV

Dear Lord,

Today I feel a bit uncertain about how to approach Your throne with my many troubles. I've prayed and prayed and things are not changing, not feeling better. It is my hope and desire to stand firm in my faith, to keep coming to You each day with the things that trouble me, but I need Your help. I need You to anoint my heart with Your Spirit and give me even a glimpse of Your face so that I can stay strong and persevere.

Please wrap Your arms around me and give me a fresh infusion of hope and faith and an honest spirit. Help me to take my eyes off the things that trouble me and put them squarely on You. Grant that as I focus on You, peace would prevail for every circumstance that concerns me.

Thank You for hearing my prayers and for keeping me close to Your heart. Thank You for being with me even in the darkness and holding me up in the light of Your love.

Amen.

In Light of Birthday Candles

*"Lord, remind me how brief my time on earth will be.
Remind me that my days are numbered—how fleeting my life is."*

Psalm 39:4 nlt

Dear heavenly Father,

Every time I light another birthday candle, I'm reminded that my days on earth are all in Your hand, numbered, and sure. I thank You for each of the days You grant me to be near my family and the people I love. Thank You for the opportunities I have to share my heart with others and to shine even a fragile light into the darkness.

Today, even though it is not my birthday, I want to be reminded again that every moment counts, that everything I do is important to the kingdom because that is why You put me here on earth. Help me to use my time wisely and well, and forgive me when I waste precious hours that could be used to serve You better.

Keep me close to You always. May all those who draw near to You today have an even greater desire to make whatever time they have on this earth a time of joy and blessing to others.

Amen.

Pray without Ceasing!

. . . .

Rejoice always, pray continually, give thanks in all circumstances; for this is God's will for you in Christ Jesus.
1 THESSALONIANS 5:16–18 NIV

Dear Lord,

I wonder what it means to pray continually, without ceasing. I pray often, and I do seek Your face and listen for Your voice in the things I do, but I'm sure I don't pray continually. I ask, Lord, for Your help to be a more intentional person of prayer. I ask that I might do a better job of showing You my gratitude for all You give me, for all You do to offer me an abundant life.

When the circumstances I face are difficult, or when the steps I need to take feel uncertain, please draw even closer to me, helping me to feel Your presence and know You are with me whatever life may bring. I rejoice that You have blessed me in more ways than I can ever count and that because of Jesus, You always make my steps firm and secure. I thank You that You are with me continually.

I pray for my family and friends and for whatever may weigh on their hearts and minds today. Thank You for being with each of us in all circumstances.

Amen.

An Agreeable Heart

. . . .

*I appeal to you, brothers and sisters, in the name of our
Lord Jesus Christ, that all of you agree with one another
in what you say and that there be no divisions among you,
but that you be perfectly united in mind and thought.*

1 CORINTHIANS 1:10 NIV

Dear Lord,

Sometimes it feels like no one agrees with anyone else in the world. Every person and every group has an opinion, and many people voice those opinions loudly across any channel of communication they can find. I feel the tension at work among my peers as each person takes a stand on the issue of the day, or even in my own home as my family members look at all sides of a question from different angles.

It's confusing to me. I pray that You would help me to have a discerning spirit in these things and in situations that cause me to feel like I'm out of harmony or I've missed the point. I pray to be united in my home and family and in our efforts to love each other and the people we connect with throughout the day.

Lord, all around the world is a spirit of disconnection and disunity. Please help us to unite under Your banner and treat each other with respect and love. Help us to be united in thought, word, and deed according to Your guidance.

Amen.

Spoiler Alert: God Loves You!

Therefore, as God's chosen people, holy and dearly loved,
clothe yourselves with compassion, kindness,
humility, gentleness and patience.

COLOSSIANS 3:12 NIV

Father in heaven,

Ever since Jesus came to live in my heart, I've been aware of Your love for me. My confession, though, is that I don't always keep that in the forefront of my mind. I don't always trust that it's true or that I even deserve Your great love. I don't always behave as though I'm a beloved child of God. That grieves my heart.

Help me to be more like You, showing genuine compassion for those in need or those who are suffering. Help me to speak kindly to everyone I meet throughout the day no matter how tired I might be or how unsettled I might feel about my own personal life. Help me to be clothed in humility, able to see Your Spirit in others.

Father, more than anything, I pray to honor the love You have for me. I pray that I will shine Your light with great joy and that I will be a good example of what it means to live in Your love. Bless everyone who knows You, and help all of us to be gentle to each other. Help all of us to live as though we truly understand the phrase "God loves you."

Amen.

Fail Today, Fly Tomorrow!

*My flesh and my heart may fail, but God is
the strength of my heart and my portion forever.*
PSALM 73:26 NIV

Dear Lord,

When I have a heavy heart because of something I've done, or something that I feel may disappoint You, I know that the best thing to do is just come before You and confess those feelings. I need to share my failures with You so that I can rejoice with You in my successes. I need to be honest with You and with myself because only You can give me wings to fly.

Today I place at the foot of the cross all those things I regret having done, and I seek Your forgiveness. I also ask Your help in letting them go and moving on to do better things. Guard me and guide me when temptations try to lure me in or when I move too quickly toward something I should have considered more carefully.

Help all Your children today who come to You with penitent hearts, knowing their failures full well, grieving over the ways they've let You down, and then help them rise again into a new day with lighter hearts toward a brighter tomorrow. Thank You for Your steadfast mercy and grace.

Amen.

The Heart of Faith

*Live in the right way, serve God, have faith, love,
patience, and gentleness. Fight the good fight of faith,
grabbing hold of the life that continues forever.*

1 TIMOTHY 6:11–12 NCV

Heavenly Father,

In my heart of hearts, I always hope to live the right way, to do the things that please You and bring peace to my soul. I hope to treat others with everyday kindness and love. You have taught me these things since the very beginning.

Help me now, Father, to continue to fight the good fight of faith. Help me to hold on for dear life when the news of the day assaults my weary mind with all the horrible things taking place around the world. Hold me close when I see the suffering on the faces of innocent people caught in the middle of some political battle that devastates their homeland.

Help me to care about others so much that when they suffer, I suffer, too, because we are all in this life together, bonded by the work of our Creator. Grant me patience as I look out at the world, and give me a deeper sense of what it means to be a person of faith. I know that no matter how bleak the world may appear, You are the only one in control and You have all things in Your hand. I pray for Your children everywhere.

Amen.

Prayer Is a Willingness of the Heart

*"I will give them a desire to respect me completely,
and I will put inside them a new way of thinking. I will
take out the stubborn heart of stone from their bodies,
and I will give them an obedient heart of flesh."*

EZEKIEL 11:19 NCV

Dear Lord,

It shakes me up a bit when I consider the ways I've had a stubborn heart, one that has been too stony to listen to You, or one that has walked on without You so I could do whatever I pleased. When I take that approach to life, things begin to fall down around me, and before I know it, I'm crying to You again about why my life doesn't feel like it's getting anywhere. Why do I look to You when I've caused my own misery?

You must laugh at my foolishness, knowing full well I'll be back on my knees in the future. From today on, I ask You to help me stay on the path You've set—the one that is directed by Your love—and then grant me the willingness to follow. I ask that You give me a willing heart that I may not only please You but help to fulfill my divine purpose for even being on this earth.

Lord, You know me better than anyone in the world will ever be able to know me. Please help me to desire a softer heart, the kind You can mold and shape and develop into sweet oneness with You. I pray that You will bless me with a heart that is totally committed to You and overflowing with peace.

Thank You for loving me and creating a willing heart within me.

Amen.

The Purposes of God's Heart

. . . .

But the plans of the LORD stand firm forever,
the purposes of his heart through all generations.
PSALM 33:11 NIV

God of heaven,

Thank You for the gift of prayer, the chance to talk with You whenever I please. When I think about the possibility of being able to come straight to Your throne anytime I have a question or a fear or a doubt, it overwhelms me. I know that You offer me the chance to talk with You because of Your beloved Son, the very one who has given each of us our purpose and blessing of eternal life.

Help me not to just think about myself but to think about Your purpose for my life and the work You want me to do. Give me a greater desire to fulfill the purposes of Your heart so that generations after me will know You and be freely able to talk with You as well.

Lord, I am grateful to You for my life, my health, my home, my work, and my family. There is nothing You have denied me, and You have gifted me with talents that I can share. I pray today for all of us who seek to do Your will here on earth. Grant us wisdom and kindheartedness, and fill us with Your Spirit to bring Your purposes to fruition for the good of all humankind. Thank You for Your unending love.

Amen.

Counting Your Blessings

* *

*"May the LORD bless you and keep you. May the
LORD show you his kindness and have mercy on you.
May the LORD watch over you and give you peace."*

NUMBERS 6:24–26 NCV

Dear Lord,

Thank You that with each sunrise I can start again to remember Your blessings from days gone by and look forward to Your blessings right now. Thank You for all You do to extend kindness and mercy and peace to my heart so that my days are full and joyful.

Forgive me when I don't acknowledge all You've done to give me the life I have—a life filled with treasures beyond measure. Thank You for answering my prayers and for shining a light on my path so I know where to go and what to do in every circumstance. You inspire my heart, and I know I would be nothing without You.

Father, please watch over those who seek You today, and fill their hearts with Your peace. Help them to trust You and see Your hand at work in all they do. Remind each person of all they have because of Your grace and mercy so they will never tire of counting their blessings. When I count mine, Lord, I always start with You.

Amen.

Traffic Jam Prayers

But, LORD, don't be far away.
You are my strength; hurry to help me.
PSALM 22:19 NCV

Dear heavenly Father,

When I look at my to-do list, hurrying here and there to accomplish each task, I sometimes forget the most important step in the process. I forget to start with You, seeking Your guidance and Your help with getting things done and, more than that, checking with You to see which things even belong on the list.

Usually, when I'm trying so hard to make each minute count, scurrying around, running as fast as I can, I find that even the world seems to conspire against me. I find myself in a traffic jam going absolutely nowhere, watching the minutes and seconds tick by while nothing gets done.

My traffic jam moments give me the chance to do what I should have done in the first place—spend time with You. Inching my way along the highway of life, I can turn to You and listen for Your voice. I can seek Your best for me and be at peace with what You would have me accomplish.

I pray, Father, for all those who need to start their day with You, that they would not wait to be in a traffic jam or a long line at a checkout somewhere before they pause to put everything on their to-do lists in Your hands. Help us to slow down and wait for You to guide us.

Amen.

A Forgiving Heart

*Can I forgive people who cheat others
with wrong weights and scales?*
MICAH 6:11 NCV

Dear Lord,

In my efforts to grow more like You, it is always my hope to be considerate and forgiving when it comes to others. I want to be compassionate and loving, willing to help when I can.

I struggle, though, when I see injustice happening anywhere in the world. I feel reluctant to forgive those who intentionally deceive or hurt others. I grow weary of trying to give them the benefit of the doubt when it is so clear that their behavior or their way of doing business is not Your way.

Today, I pray for those who are engaged in any effort to deceive others rather than shine a light on the truth of what they do. I ask that You would convict their spirits and their hearts so that they would seek forgiveness for the wrong they intended and draw near to You for guidance and mercy. I pray that You would protect people from the deceivers of the world, guard their hearts and their lives, and cause temptation and evil to flee from them.

If there is any deception in my heart, Lord, please cast a light on it so that I may seek Your forgiveness and walk more closely with You. Renew me and give me a forgiving heart for all I do.

Amen.

A Troubled Heart

"See, O LORD, that I am in distress; my soul is troubled; my heart is overturned within me, for I have been very rebellious."

LAMENTATIONS 1:20 NKJV

Dear Lord,

You know me. In fact, You know me better than I even know myself. You know what makes me tick and what excites me. You know what motivates me to keep trying and what causes me to struggle and even think of giving up. I thank You that You have loved me for so long and that You continue to teach me Your ways.

Lord, I'm most distressed when I realize that I, too, can be rebellious, that I can walk away from You and think I can handle life all on my own. It scares me to even imagine what I would do without You, and so I don't truly understand those times when I figure it's better to go it alone. It's never better to be without You!

Help me to be honest with myself. Help me to be willing to confess my sins and my rebellious heart and misguided ways. Forgive me when I lose sight of the goal and the work that You have for me. My heart is troubled when I do those things. Bless each person today, Lord, who realizes how much they need You and how important it is to stay honest with You all the time. Help us to share Your love in all we do.

Amen.

Nowhere to Hide

"God watches where people go; he sees every step
they take. There is no dark place or deep shadow
where those who do evil can hide from him."

JOB 34:21–22 NCV

Dear Lord,

I know You are always in our midst, always near to us. You see who we are and what we are. You notice the things we do to follow Your ways and the places in our hearts where we still deceive ourselves. You know the efforts we make to do better and to seek Your will for our lives.

I ask today, Lord, that You would know me, that You would teach me about the places I try to hide from You and from others. I pray that You would raise me up to a new standard of humility and honor. Help me to surrender those things to You that I try so hard to hide. I know there is nothing I can keep from You; and more than that, there is nothing that I want to keep from You.

I remember the story of how Adam and Eve hid in the garden when they discovered they were naked, when they realized that they had done something wrong. They didn't want You to know. They didn't want You to see them. I feel like that when I do wrong, too. Forgive those things about me. Forgive those places where I try to run away. Strengthen and renew me. Grant me a heart that is totally surrendered to Your love and care. Clothe me in Your righteousness.

Amen.

When You Are a Little Bit Angel

Whoever gives to others will get richer;
those who help others will themselves be helped.
PROVERBS 11:25 NCV

Heavenly Father,

Today, I am feeling blessed by all the people who have reached out to me during various trials in my life. These are the people You sent my way to offer me a hand and help me carry the load, the burden I could not manage all by myself. I thank You for the people who have been like angels to me, who have ministered to me and blessed me more than they know.

Remind me of those people often so that I might pray for them. Remind me, too, so I might be even more like them, doing the same for others as they did for me. Help me to have more compassion for my neighbors and friends, to pray for their well-being and to lend a hand when they need me. Help me to become part of their solution when the problems of life become overwhelming.

We are each of us able to be angels to each other when we choose to be. I am so grateful for all those people in my life, and I lift them up to You. I know that my life is richer when I give to others, so I pray to be a blessing wherever You call me to lend a hand.

Amen.

Madcap Heart

. . . .

*Then all the people went away to eat and drink, to send
some of their food to others, and to celebrate with great joy.*

NEHEMIAH 8:12 NCV

Dear Lord,

Thank You for giving me days when my heart is light and I simply feel like celebrating my life and all You've done to fill my heart with joy. Because of You, I have a clearer understanding of my own purpose and the ways I can be Your hands and feet in the world. You have given me a vision of what I do best and how I can use my gifts and talents to serve You and to help others along the way. That alone is worth a celebration, and so I offer You my thanks and praise.

I pray for all those who do not yet understand Your will for their lives and what Your dream is for them. Help them to know You in a way that causes their hearts to bubble up with joy and thanksgiving. Help all Your children to know Your goodness and love and to do a happy dance for the things You've shown them. I pray their joy will continue and overflow and that Your blessings will be poured out upon them all.

Thank You for Your great love for me and for providing for me in every way. Thank You for giving me a life that is worth celebrating all the time.

Amen.

In a Heartbeat!

*Listen to me and save me quickly. Be my
rock of protection, a strong city to save me.*
Psalm 31:2 NCV

Dear Father in heaven,

It disappoints me when I do things that are just plain foolish.
I look at my actions or my reactions to something, and I instantly
know that I was wrong. I regret it in a heartbeat, and I wish I could
take it all back or get a do-over. Do You give do-overs? I hope
so, because today I need one, and I ask for Your help. Just like
the psalmist, I pray You will come quickly to save me and be my
protector. Sometimes I need You to protect me even from myself.

Help me get back on course. Forgive me for falling behind,
and restore me to Your love and mercy and grace. Thank You for
loving me so much that You are willing to pick me up when I fall,
brush me off, make me clean, and give me a chance to start all
over again. What a mess I'd be without You! You are my Lord and
Savior, and I know I stumble through life each time I take my eyes
off You—each time I choose to go in my own direction.

Bless my life today, along with all those who stumble and fall.
Return us all quickly to Your side and grant us Your mercy and
peace. Keep us close to You with every heartbeat!

Amen.

Heart-Shaped Words

*The words of a good person give life,
like a fountain of water.*
PROVERBS 10:11 NCV

Dear Lord,

It's funny how words stick in our minds and replay themselves over and over. If they are good words, we remember them fondly. If they are harsh words, we sometimes never get past them because they haunt us like ghosts we can't leave behind.

Lord, You still speak here on earth; and when people listen, lives are changed and blessings are created. Steps are taken in a good direction for the sake of Your kingdom and for all that You want to happen. Your words create life and make us strong.

Help me to remember how important the words I speak can be. Remind me to be tender and compassionate, willing to give more than I receive, continually seeking the good of the person to whom I am speaking. Help me to stir the waters of joy in their heart by the good words I speak so that anytime those words are recalled in the future, they will bubble forth like a fountain giving life and strength.

Help all of us to use our words wisely when we speak to one another.

Amen.

A Divided Heart

"No one can serve two masters. Either you will hate the one
and love the other, or you will be devoted to the one and
despise the other. You cannot serve both God and money."

MATTHEW 6:24 NIV

Dear Lord,

It is never my intention to get so focused on making a living or on making money that I forget to pay attention to You. I know that all that I have comes from Your hand, and I am blessed to receive what I need from Your mercy and Your bounty.

Sometimes, though, I get caught up in the stress and worry of trying to make more money simply to cover the bills that never end and to take care of the basic needs that are part of living here on earth. Today I ask for Your grace and Your help to keep the proper balance between what I must do to make a living and what I want to do to live well in Your eyes. Help me to start with You—reading Your Word and listening to Your voice—no matter what else I do each day. Help me to seek You first no matter what else needs to be done.

I pray for all the people I know who feel like they are continually scrambling to make ends meet, barely scraping enough together to manage each day. I ask that You would help each of us to see that You provide for our daily bread and that You have our future in Your hands. Draw near to us so we can come to You each day and feel Your gracious presence. Thank You, Lord, for giving us a heart to serve only You.

Amen.

God Sees Me

She gave this name to the LORD who spoke to her:
"You are the God who sees me," for she said,
"I have now seen the One who sees me."

GENESIS 16:13 NIV

Dear God,

Sometimes, like Hagar in the Bible, I feel like I'm walking alone in the wilderness, wondering if You see me. I do my best to survive the ups and downs of life and to stay on the path that seems right. Even so, I often find myself praying that I would feel that You were closer to me, able to help me get over the hurdles I face.

The truth is that You are with me, always. You walk beside me in the dark hours when I don't know which way to turn. You reach out for me to offer me shelter and keep me safe. You embrace my heart and mind and bless me with a glimpse of what is to come.

Help me to raise my eyes to see You so that my heart embraces all that You have for me. Help me to trust You when I'm in a desert of despair and don't know what steps to take next. Help me to understand that I am not alone, no matter where I may wander, because You see me all the time.

I pray, Lord, that I will see You, too, knowing firsthand that I am in Your care whatever the day may bring.

Amen.

Centered in Peace

May the God of hope fill you with all joy and peace
as you trust in him, so that you may overflow
with hope by the power of the Holy Spirit.

ROMANS 15:13 NIV

Father in heaven,

We don't live in a peaceful world. Every day we are bombarded with news of devastation. . .from mudslides, to the plight of homeless people, to the horrors of wars. We try to go on and hope for the best, only to find ourselves quietly wondering where it will all lead and if there is anything at all we can do to better the situation. It is never ending, and nothing can make a sustainable difference except You.

I pray for all people who seek Your peace. Give them a break from the uproar and chaos that others would cast upon them. Give them peaceful hearts and minds, and help them to share their hope and gratitude in You with those around them. Help them to be centered in peace in ways that they have not been able to achieve for days on end.

You know what we need. You know how important it is for us to be calm and quiet and still and able to rest in Your care. I pray for Your peace, Your presence, Your love to permeate the globe so that everywhere we turn we would know You are there. Bless us with real peace, the kind that can only come from Your loving Holy Spirit.

Amen.

Appreciation and Praise

*Let the message of Christ dwell among you richly as
you teach and admonish one another with all wisdom
through psalms, hymns, and songs from the Spirit,
singing to God with gratitude in your hearts.*

COLOSSIANS 3:16 NIV

Dear Lord,

How often do we sing, "Praise God, from whom all blessings flow; praise Him, all creatures here below; praise Him above, ye heavenly host; praise Father, Son, and Holy Ghost?"

Something about that song and those words always gives me a sense of deep-down joy. I know in my heart that You are there and that I am singing to You, and I mean every word. I praise You, Lord, and I know that from Your hand all blessings flow. I know I do not have one thing in my life that You did not give me out of Your generous and loving spirit. I know You see me—yes, *me*—way down here in the little town I live in, smack-dab on this beautiful landscape You designed so long ago.

Today I pray for all the people who call upon Your name and who believe that You are in control and that You know their hearts more than anything or anyone ever could. I pray that all of us will lift our hearts in song to You. I pray that people everywhere may shout with joy for all You have done and all You will do in their lives. May each person acknowledge You in song and let the message of Christ dwell in their heart like the sweet fragrance of springtime flowers.

Amen.

At the Heart of Forgiveness

. . . .

Bear with each other and forgive one another
if any of you has a grievance against someone.
Forgive as the Lord forgave you.
COLOSSIANS 3:13 NIV

Father of forgiveness,

You know, Lord, I think I'm good at being a forgiver. As far as I know, I'm not holding a grudge toward anyone, and I'm not withholding my friendship from someone because of a past grievance. I tend to think I'm doing okay in the forgiving department.

But then You remind me of those that I have forgotten from days gone by, those that I might yet seek forgiveness from. I ask Your forgiveness for any that I have offended, unwittingly perhaps, but still the fault is mine. You also remind me that there is one person I'm not good at forgiving at all, and that person is me!

I seek Your help, Lord, to ask forgiveness from anyone I know I've hurt in some way because of something I did or something I omitted to do. I ask that You would also help me to forgive myself for the things I've done that grieve my heart and Yours.

I know You are willing to forgive me when I offer You a contrite heart. Today, with my whole heart, I seek Your forgiveness and Your love. Shape me and mold me into the person You want me to be.

Amen.

With My Whole Heart

*I will praise you, LORD, with all my heart; I will tell of all
the marvelous things you have done. I will be filled with joy
because of you. I will sing praises to your name, O Most High.*

PSALM 9:1–2 NLT

Dear Lord,

I love the idea of praising You with my whole heart. I try to imagine what it must be like for all of those gathered around Your throne to be able to be so closely connected to You, so energized by Your love that all they can think of are ways to offer You praise. It's such a beautiful picture to hold.

Help me to remember that You are always close to me. You bless me with Your strength and energy wherever I am. You offer me the chance to share in the beauty You created all over the planet, if only I have eyes to see and grasp what You have done. Help me to tell others of Your love and sing with gusto when I'm in the car or in the shower or anyplace at all.

Lord, You have done marvelous things, and my heart is full of love and joy and praise for You. Help me to continue to see Your hand in all I do and shine a light so that others might see You and give You the glory You so richly deserve.

Thank You for loving me so much. I'm singing to You now with my whole heart!

Amen.

Those Deep Thoughts

. . . .

Yet you know me, LORD; you see me
and test my thoughts about you.
JEREMIAH 12:3 NIV

Dear Father in heaven,

Thank You for knowing me so well. Thank You for forgiving me when a stray thought crosses my mind that appalls me, a thought that is out of character or not based on who I am or who I want to be before You. Sometimes I don't even know why a thought enters my mind that I didn't beckon, or why I feel stubborn about something I would normally not resist, or why I am not willing to pray even when my heart seeks You.

Crazy thoughts come, perhaps to all of us. I ask You to guard my thoughts and create a clean heart within me so that I might think only loving and precious thoughts toward You and those around me. Help me to think of the good You do and the ways You so willingly show up in my life. Help me to tell others of Your amazing goodness and truth. You know I have so many stories to tell.

Lord, I know that my thoughts are not Your thoughts, and I'm so grateful for that. I only ask that You would continue to shape my thoughts so that I can reflect more of You and less of me. Help me pass any test that might come into my thoughts so that what I think, what I do, and what I speak to others are all pleasing to You. Bless my deepest thoughts, and open my heart to know You better.

Amen.

Inside Out

. . . .

May the words of my mouth and the meditation of my heart
be pleasing to you, O LORD, my rock and my redeemer.
PSALM 19:14 NLT

Dear Lord,

You have said that what comes out of a person is based on what is inside a person. From a good person's heart come good things. From a bad person's heart come bad things. It seems simple enough. With the psalmist, I pray that the words of my mouth would only come from the good things You have already placed in my heart. I pray that I would not speak ill of any person or create an atmosphere of chaos in any situation by the things I say.

We all know what it is like to have someone speak unkindly of us and how it breaks our hearts when others think badly of us because they have listened to gossip and not waited to know the truth. Let me be someone who refuses to spread rumors or repeat information that isn't mine to share. Let me only share the light of Your love through the words I speak.

Make my heart more tender toward You and toward others in my life. Help me to lift the spirits of everyone I meet with good words—words that are pleasing to You, my rock and my redeemer.

Amen.

Strong and Brave

I love you, LORD; you are my strength.
PSALM 18:1 NLT

Dear Lord,

It takes courage to live in the world today. I guess it has always been that way; but our potential to destroy ourselves is more apparent all the time, and it seems that most of us feel there is little we can do about the problems. Terror strikes at our hearts even when we don't want to allow it in.

I ask that You would help us to know Your peace and Your love and Your strength to such a degree that nothing can undermine it. The news broadcast of the day cannot shake us. The newspapers and podcasts and blogs of the moment declaring gloom and doom cannot keep us down. Nothing can separate us from the love of Christ, and nothing can keep us from Your protection and care. I ask that You would fill us with a spirit of peace so we all try harder to simply get along.

Lord, I ask that You would not let me contribute in any way to those things that cause dissension and bring heartache to others. Help me to mend fences and tear down walls that keep people apart. Help me to show Your strength to those who need You as much as I do. Thank You for Your steadfast love and faithfulness. You are indeed my strength, and I love You.

Amen.

Kindhearted You

. . . .

The LORD God is like a sun and shield; the LORD gives us
kindness and honor. He does not hold back anything
good from those whose lives are innocent.

PSALM 84:11 NCV

Heavenly Father,

I pray for those who are dear to my heart today. I pray that
You would be a sun and a shield for them—keeping them warm
by Your grace and protecting them wherever they are. I pray that
You would not withhold anything from those who do all they can
to live for You and who trust You.

As for me, I ask that You would protect my heart and mind,
causing me to be more kindhearted to Your children everywhere
and more willing to surrender myself to Your desire for my life.

Help me to shine a light of encouragement to people in my
own household who struggle with life. Grant me words of wisdom
and compassion so that I can understand what their needs might
be and support them with love in the same way that You so often
support me. Help me to be willing to live a heart-shaped life at
home, or at work, or anywhere that You call me to be today.

Bless those who seek You; shield them with Your strong arms,
and grant that all good things might come into their lives that are
in line with Your will and purpose.

Amen.

No Day Like Today!

- -

This is the day the LORD has made;
we will rejoice and be glad in it.

PSALM 118:24 NKJV

Dear Lord,

I once read a quote from Emily Dickinson that said, "We turn not older with years, but newer every day."

I like that idea, especially as I get older myself. It's nice to think that with each day I have reason for more hope and that my spirit is refreshed. It is wonderful to know I don't have to carry yesterday's burdens into today, because You designed me to carry only one day's burdens at a time. You designed me to live in the present and to live in Your presence.

I celebrate this day, knowing You are in control and that there will never be another day like this one again. No matter how I choose to spend this day, or how You and I together create this day, it is only going to happen right now. With that in mind, Lord, help me to use my time wisely and to spend this day well. Help me to work and love and laugh and create a day that is meaningful and one that is a blessing to those around me.

Help me to use this day for what it is: a gift to my life. Bless all the people everywhere who seek Your presence and rejoice in the day You've given them.

Amen.

A Little Baby's Breath

*"The Spirit of God has made me, and the
breath of the Almighty gives me life."*

JOB 33:4 NKJV

Dear Lord,

I love the little white flowers that are often used to highlight the beauty of roses or other brightly colored floral bouquets. Baby's breath is simple and sweet and delicate and adds a little extra white light to the flowers around it. It sets them apart and makes a difference to their character and design.

Sometimes I think of Your Spirit as being like that for me. Your Spirit is the best part of me; it is the thing that makes everything else about me more beautiful. Your Spirit helps me to breathe more easily, keeping me balanced and strong. I know that without Your Spirit to enhance my life, I would not do well. In fact, I would have no light to share with others.

Thank You for giving me the breath of life through Your Son, Jesus. Thank You for shaping my heart and mind so I can breathe You in and bloom with joy. I pray that the breath of Your Spirit will fill all the people I love and give them life beyond measure. With every breath, I give You thanks and praise.

Amen.

A Prayerful Heart

But you are a chosen people, a royal priesthood, a holy nation, God's special possession, that you may declare the praises of him who called you out of darkness into his wonderful light.

1 PETER 2:9 NIV

Dear Lord,

It occurs to me that one of the ways we recognize and give credit to each other is simply by sharing what someone did. When people we love accomplish a big task and we feel proud of them for it, we share that fact with others. We are so pleased that we'll tell anyone who will listen. If we get a hole in one on the golf course, the first thing we do is tell others; or if we bake a perfect apple pie, we're eager for others to sample it and share in our joy.

I wonder if You feel the same way when I talk about You. When I tell someone what You have done to make my life better, how You showed up in the nick of time when I was in deep despair, or how You opened a door for me that I could never have opened myself, I'm giving You praise. I'm letting people know that the God of my heart, the Creator of the universe, still takes a personal interest in His children. I'm so excited that I simply must let people know.

Lord, I am grateful for all You do, and nothing gives me greater joy than sharing my stories of Your divine intervention with anybody who will listen. Thank You for Your love and Your willingness to sustain me in every area of life.

Thank You for giving me plenty of chances to share Your stories.

Amen.

The Apple of Your Eye

Keep me as the apple of your eye;
hide me in the shadow of your wings.
PSALM 17:8 NIV

Dear Guardian of my soul,

I know that I need You. I need You from the moment I wake up each morning to the moment I drift off to dreamland at night. I need You to watch over me and help me with every choice I make at home, at work, or at play. I need You to guide my thoughts and my actions, helping me to be kind to and have compassion for those around me. Sometimes I need You to simply be with me in the stillness, hiding me from those who would cause me any kind of harm.

Today, I ask You to keep guarding Your children and helping them to understand that they are important to You. Help them to know that You hold them close, in the shadow of Your wings, watching over them because each one is the apple of Your eye. I pray that You will keep them from harm, remove them from temptation, and deliver them safely wherever they go.

Lord, we all need You every hour of the day, and we pray that You will always be near, ready to help us and ready to embrace us as we walk our separate paths and do the work You've called each of us to do. Thank You for keeping us safely tucked beneath Your wings.

Amen.

As I Grow

. . . .

But I am like an olive tree growing in God's Temple.
I trust God's love forever and ever.
PSALM 52:8 NCV

Dear Lord,

I love the way You make things grow. You have one person plant seeds, or another person water crops, but You alone know all the secrets of how and why things grow. I love the idea that I am like a strong and rugged tree growing in Your garden or any place You send me here on earth. Just knowing I'm on the grounds You tend makes me happy. Only You can provide the perfect soil and light and nutrients for my life so I can develop strength of character and grow more capable in every way.

Thank You for making sure I have all I need to flourish. Bless the people in my family who are growing stronger each day because of the ways You nurture them and the love we share together. Bless all the families of the earth who seek Your face and strive to grow closer to You, standing tall like olive trees and trusting in Your love forever.

I trust in Your love and in Your strength and kindness, for without You I would simply wither away. Without You I could never flourish and blossom. Bless all those who desire to grow well and live to accomplish Your purposes.

Amen.

It's a Beautiful World!

Sing to the LORD and praise his name; every day tell how he saves us. Tell the nations of his glory; tell all peoples the miracles he does, because the LORD is great; he should be praised at all times.

PSALM 96:2–4 NCV

Dear Lord,

When I think about what You do for me every day, I can't help but give You praise. I want You to know that I'm grateful every hour for Your saving grace and mercy. You are the one who allows the sun to rise so that a new day dawns. You are the one who hears my heart about the things that worry me or the things that make my day eventful one way or another.

You are always there for me; and whether I acknowledge Your fullness, Your guidance, and Your hand on my life or whether I don't, You stand with me. You create little miracles throughout the day that give me joy or greater understanding of Your love for me. You are my protector and my guardian, and so I thank You.

Help bring to mind all that You've done so that I might share Your goodness with others, encouraging their walk with You and helping them to have hope in Your goodness and steadfast love. Help me to share Your love with all my heart, whatever I may do today. It's a beautiful world anytime You are near.

Amen.

What the Heart Sees

. . . .

The LORD looks down from heaven and sees the whole human
race. From his throne he observes all who live on the earth.
He made their hearts, so he understands everything they do.

PSALM 33:13–15 NLT

Father in heaven,

I pray that when You look down on me today, You would see a heart that loves You and a heart that longs to know more of You. I pray that You would encourage me to stand strong for You so that my family and friends, my neighbors and coworkers, and all the people I meet today would see Your light shining through my eyes.

I pray that I won't disappoint You in any of the things I do, but that I will radiate Your presence and the gifts of Your Spirit to those who need You as much as I do. Help me to be more of the person You designed me to be for Your sake and not for my own. Grant that I might fulfill my purpose while I am here on earth so that when I return to You someday, we can rejoice in the work we did together.

As You see me faltering, help me to grow and mature in Your love and give me a soft heart for You, for others, and especially for those who draw near to You in hope. Strengthen all those who seek to understand Your will for their lives and who hope to find the path to a more meaningful life. Help each of us to feel Your presence in our hearts today. Help each of us to make You proud.

Amen.

He Sees Your Heart

. . . .

"Worship and serve him with your whole heart and a willing mind. For the LORD sees every heart and knows every plan and thought. If you seek him, you will find him."
1 CHRONICLES 28:9 NLT

Dear Lord,

Sometimes I'm not very proud of my every plan and thought. I know I do not serve You with my whole heart or demonstrate that I have a willing mind. I know that when I'm distant from You, it's me who went away and not You.

I confess this to You because I know it's the truth. There's more, though. Other times, I do my best to love You and serve You with my whole heart and with a willing mind. I look to You to guide me and lead me and help me to be all that You want me to be. I love that You see me "heart first" and that You are so close to me.

I pray to be more of the person who seeks You and who intentionally offers You my whole heart and my willing mind. Help me to be someone You can be proud of. . .someone who is prepared to lead others closer to Your light. I know that when my heart is open to You and when my mind embraces all that You are, I can do a better job of shining Your light.

Thank You for seeing my heart and knowing that I seek to serve You and love You with all that I am. I pray that all of us who seek You would find You today.

Amen.

A Courageous Heart

. . . .

I will bless the LORD who guides me; even at night my
heart instructs me. I know the LORD is always with me.
I will not be shaken, for he is right beside me.
PSALM 16:7–8 NLT

Dear Father in heaven,

When the moon fills the night sky and I am fast asleep, I know You are there and that You are keeping me safe. You watch over me and give me peace. You also continue to teach me, giving me dreams that will help me understand something I've been faced with during my waking hours, or something that I need to see more clearly concerning my life choices or the things that vex my spirit.

Nothing comforts me more than knowing You are always by my side and that I don't have to wonder if You'll be there when a crisis happens or when I feel uncertain about my next steps. I know that whatever happens to me, You work things out for my good because You love me so much.

Bless the dreams of all the people I love. Help them sleep in peace each night, and embrace them with Your presence. Let them know that You are always near and that nothing will ever happen to them that will be a surprise to You. You watch over them for their good, and You guide their hearts and minds through the night and again through the day. Thank You for Your kind and generous Spirit.

Amen.

The Greatest of These Is Love

*And now abide faith, hope, love, these three;
but the greatest of these is love.*

1 Corinthians 13:13 NKJV

Dear Lord,

I've tried to respond to Your commands to love with my whole heart. I've tried to understand more of what it means to love You and what it means for You to love me. I've tried to look with integrity at myself and my willingness to love others. Sometimes I've done a pretty good job at those things. . .and sometimes I haven't.

When I go to Your Word, I discover more of Your commands about ways to love others. You remind me to speak kindly to those around me. You help me see the importance of giving guidance and good advice. You've shown me ways to be generous to those less fortunate than I am. You've even said I should pray for my enemies.

The list of ways to love others is virtually unending. Perhaps that's because Your love for me and for all Your children is unending as well. You have shown me repeatedly that You care about me—all of me, my head, my heart, my mind, and my spirit. You know me like no one else can. Please keep guiding me in the ways that soften my heart, and help me to be more generous and open to loving You and loving others. Help me to stretch my thinking, even if it means I will be a little uncomfortable with ways I can learn to love others better. You are my guide and my example of real love every day.

Amen.

Distress Calls

"See, O LORD, that I am in distress; my soul is troubled;
my heart is overturned within me."
LAMENTATIONS 1:20 NKJV

Dear God,

When my heart is troubled, I don't always know which way to turn. I'm weighed down by those sins of commission or even the ones of omission, knowing in my heart of hearts that I have done things that aren't pleasing to You. I know that my soul hurts and my heart is indeed "overturned" within me.

Whatever the distress of my life might be, I know that You alone are my advocate, that You see me and love me and want to help me do better. I pray that You would take me by the hand and lead me to the places I need to go to serve You in every way.

Your servants are all over the globe, and they seek Your face. Today, I ask that You would shine Your light on each of them—and on me—so that we might all be examples of Your love. Our world is in distress; and everywhere we look, people are in trouble. Help me and others who believe in You to do what we can to be a source of encouragement and compassion.

Thank You for hearing our prayers and being willing to remain steadfastly by our sides, because You are the strength and shield of our lives and the best portion and example of what love is all about.

Amen.

A Radiant Heart

"Look around you. People are gathering and coming to you. Your sons are coming from far away, and your daughters are coming with them. When you see them, you will shine with happiness; you will be excited and full of joy."

ISAIAH 60:4–5 NCV

O Lord,

I love it when my family and friends gather around me. There's nothing like a good family feast, some warm conversation, and the blessing of genuine, loving interaction to give us a sense of joy. It gives us a sense of belonging and a glimpse of what it means to be in relationship with You. Families give us a chance to give and receive love.

Help us to take that feeling, that radiance, and give it a wider net. Help us to embrace people who may stand outside our family circle but who need to have the joy of good relationships and good friends. Help us to see each person we meet as someone who is Your child, Your friend, and someone who needs Your light.

The more we recognize You in each other, embrace all children as Your sons and daughters, the more we reflect You to a weary and unhappy world. Let us shine for You and share our excitement with anyone who will listen. Most of all, give us hearts to draw people into our inner circles so we can share all You have done. Expand our territories and our definitions of what it means to be family wherever we are.

Amen.

An Attitude of Gratitude

. . . .

No wonder my heart is glad, and I rejoice.
My body rests in safety.
PSALM 16:9 NLT

Dear Lord,

I like to think that I start each day with a heart filled with joy and thankfulness for all You've done for me and all that You have given me. I do show You my gratitude, but I'm sure it isn't enough. I miss more opportunities to thank You with all my heart than I ever embrace.

Open my mind to the amazing things You have done, and fill my heart with the kind of joy that overflows.

I would be lost without Jesus. You would not be able to see me or hear my prayers if it weren't for His steadfast love and faithfulness. I thank You that Jesus is standing in the gaps, those gaping holes I often leave open where I forget to give You thanks and praise. I thank You that Your Son redeemed me and works so hard to give me a softer heart, molded and shaped so I can become a better person.

I thank You that I have enough. I have a sufficient income, enough to eat, people who love me, and people who guide me. I have enough because You provide for me every single day. You are the air I breathe and the lifeblood of my existence. Thank You for Your gifts of joy, Your willingness to forgive me, save me, and mold me into being all that You know I can be.

Amen.

Bless Your Heart!

I pray also that you will have greater understanding in your heart so you will know the hope to which he has called us and that you will know how rich and glorious are the blessings God has promised his holy people.

Ephesians 1:18 NCV

Dear Father in heaven,

You are the hope of the world, and You are the only hope each of us has for all of eternity. Thank You for calling us into Your family, for giving us a portion of Your inheritance so that we may have a future and live with You forever.

You have changed us. We can no longer walk around with hearts of stone, unable or unwilling to see the needs of those around us. We cannot be blind to those who need simple words of encouragement or a few moments of warm conversation. We are living with Your promise, growing in knowledge and understanding of You all the time.

Grant that I would experience Your Spirit and shine Your light and bless those who are near me wherever I am today. Help me to be wise and full of discernment for each choice I make, especially when those choices affect the lives of others.

Bless my friends and my family. Bless my home and my work—and most of all, bless my heart to grow stronger and softer and more aware of You in all ways and for always. Help me to know Your rich and glorious blessings and freely share them in every possible way.

Amen.

Becoming More

But when a person changes and follows the Lord, that covering is taken away. The Lord is the Spirit, and where the Spirit of the Lord is, there is freedom. Our faces, then, are not covered. We all show the Lord's glory, and we are being changed to be like him. This change in us brings ever greater glory, which comes from the Lord, who is the Spirit.

2 CORINTHIANS 3:16–18 NCV

Dear Lord of glory,

A long time ago, I put my weak hand in Your strong one and asked You into my life. You came. You have taken me on quite a journey since then, teaching me things I never could have imagined, showing me things I could not have understood apart from You. You have turned Your face toward me to teach me important life lessons. I am in a continual state of gratitude and awe for the things You have done.

Today, Lord, I pray that my spirit will be aligned so completely with Yours that nothing can come between us. I pray that I will freely follow where You would lead, knowing You have my back and that I can trust You for every step we take. I pray that You would go ahead of me, guiding my efforts to become more like You in any way I can.

Following You means the old me is gone and the new me comes to You to be refreshed every morning. I need a dose of You before I go out into the world so that I can be better prepared for the day. Bless all those who come to You for strength and renewal, and help each of us to continue to seek Your face and the guidance of Your Spirit.

Amen.

Be the Light

*"You are the light that gives light to the world.
A city that is built on a hill cannot be hidden."*

MATTHEW 5:14 NCV

Dear Father in heaven,

I asked You some time ago to "let me be the light." When I asked You this, I didn't know exactly what I meant. I didn't even know if I could do it. I just knew that I wanted more of You to light me up from the inside so I could share more of You with others.

Since that time, You have blessed me with the opportunity to shine. You have sent me into some dark places to offer hope. You have moved me from one city to another to be a little beacon on a hill.

I'm grateful for Your willingness to keep teaching me about being a light in the world. I love knowing that You don't set me out there like a flood lamp, but You simply let me turn up the light in my own way and style. You guide me to do the best I can. You keep my little light from ever going out.

Help me reflect Your love so I can be the image of You that most captures the hearts of people I meet today. Help me to be not only someone who carries Your light, but someone carried by Your holy light everyplace I go. Thank You for Your generous love that sustains me and helps me become more of what You would have me be.

Amen.

A Good Heart for Others

"Do to others as you would have them do to you."

LUKE 6:31 NIV

Dear God,

I learned the Golden Rule when I was just a child. It always made perfect sense that I would seek to treat other people the same way I hoped to be treated. I thought if I was kind, then other people would be kind. The sad part is that now I've grown up, and I've discovered that kindness is simply not the rule, not always the response.

Help me respond with Your grace and mercy when others are angry or mean-spirited. Help me be an influence for kindness and for the positive good of others.

I pray today for those people who have been hurt by life or who have a need to be cruel to others. I pray that Your light would shine into their hearts and change their view of themselves, renewing a right spirit within them. I pray that You would strengthen them and give them hearts that are open to love and to understanding.

Forgive us when we violate the lives of others in ways that harm them and betray their trust. Make us aware of the ways we can make a difference in building relationships that follow the Golden Rule. You know we need our hearts to be aligned with Yours so we can understand what it means to be good to each other. I pray for Your spirit of truth and love to fill our souls today.

Amen.

I Believe in Love

> *"I give you a new command: Love each other. You must love each other as I have loved you. All people will know that you are my followers if you love each other."*
>
> JOHN 13:34–35 NCV

Dear Lord,

Your command for us to love each other seems simple in theory. Somehow in practice, it's not so easy. When I consider the difficulties that can come from trying to love others, I'm awed that You don't struggle to love me, or the rest of Your children, the way we struggle to love each other. You love us even when we don't make it easy for You. We don't show You continual respect and adoration. We don't even talk to You very often; yet You keep loving us.

Help me remember that if I'm going to love others as You love me, then I have to be willing to love them with all their flaws. I must love them when they do things that make me angry or sad. I must love them when they talk back to me or even when they ignore me. The bottom line is that I should love them because You love them.

Help me to love You better, too. Let Your light glow within me so that others can see that I belong to You and that I choose to love those You have put in my life as friends, family, or acquaintances. Help me to be a good example of what You mean when You command us to love each other.

Amen.

God Believes in All You Can Be

*But, Lord, you are a God who shows mercy
and is kind. You don't become angry quickly.
You have great love and faithfulness.*
PSALM 86:15 NCV

Dear Father in heaven,

Sometimes I shy away from talking to You. I know You are willing to give me mercy, but I feel so disappointed with myself for having done something I know grieves Your heart that I hate to face You. I ask that You would help me to seek Your face before I do those things that don't serve me or You very well. I ask that You would mold my heart and mind to desire more often to do the right thing the first time.

I thank You that You don't get angry with me quickly, but that You give me time to see what the consequences of my choices might be. You know that whatever I do, I must live with myself, and sometimes that's not easy. The truth is that my heart grieves when I give in to my weaknesses.

Today, I pray that You will renew my strength and create a clean heart within me, one that appreciates Your kindness and mercy and one that strives to be a person worthy of Your love and faithfulness. I don't want to ever be afraid to talk with You about anything.

Amen.

Believe It or Not

. . . .

Know and believe today that the LORD is God. He is God in heaven above and on the earth below. There is no other god!
DEUTERONOMY 4:39 NCV

Dear Lord,

Every day I live, You present me with a choice. You step into my life and ask if I believe You exist. You ask if I trust You alone. You ask me what activities of the day, or what thoughts from yesterday, will weigh on me so much that I'm preoccupied or willing to put those things ahead of You.

Your questions are fair, and they cause me to look at my actions. They cause me to look at my choices, to face myself in the mirror. Sometimes it appears that I have managed to allow my worries and concerns to have priority. I go to sleep with the weight of them on my mind, and I wake up with them staring me in the face once more. I turn my fears and doubts into huge boulders, obstacles that I created. Those are the obstacles that separate me from You. Those obstacles, those worries, are like man-made gods that can do nothing for me. My worries never come to my rescue. Only You can rescue me.

Father, help me to stop looking at the obstacles and focus directly on You. Align my heart with Your will so that I will truly have only one God, one guide through every circumstance in life. I believe in You, the only God of this universe!

Amen.

Where Your Heart Belongs

. . . .

You will show me the way of life, granting me the joy of your presence and the pleasures of living with you forever.

PSALM 16:11 NLT

Lord God,

Today I pray that You will share Your secrets, that You will show me the way of life. Help me to seek You with all my heart, soul, and mind so that I can truly live for You as though nothing else matters. I suspect that there is only one truth for me, and it is all about my willingness to walk with You and be connected to You.

Grant me the joy of Your presence when I do household chores or when I make a meal for my family. Give me the sense that You are with me when I do the mundane things that keep my home and my family strong.

Show me the places where I need to walk with You more closely, where I need to guard my heart against temptation, or where I need to spend more time in prayer. Help me to understand that the true pleasures of living come from You. The more I do for You, the closer I am to You and the more I recognize the joy that radiates from my toes to the smile on my face. Only the joy that You bring me can fill my heart to overflowing so that it then lights up the room when I have a chance to be with others.

Set my heart right with You today, and hold me close in all that I do.

Amen.

When Your Heart Is Suffering

*Then they sat on the ground with Job seven days
and seven nights. No one said a word to him
because they saw how much he was suffering.*

JOB 2:13 NCV

Dear Lord,

I struggle with the idea of suffering in the lives of people I love. I don't want anyone to have to suffer terrible loss or grief, or severe disappointment in love or in relationships with friends or family. I believe that You don't want any of us to suffer and that it grieves Your heart when we're in pain.

Sometimes we bring suffering upon ourselves. Job did not cause his own suffering, but he was caught in a divine struggle between good and evil. He suffered, and yet he held on to the one thing he could understand. He held on to the knowledge that You were there. Even when he couldn't feel Your presence, he trusted You were near and that You knew all that was happening to him.

I try to imagine what it was like for his friends to sit with him, taking in his suffering but not speaking a word to help. They were just present with him in his incredible grief. Teach me to be a person who is willing to simply sit with those who grieve, or sit with them and perhaps shine a light on the fact that You are there with us. Help me not assume that I must come up with the right words to try and comfort them. Help me to simply be of the right heart and the right spirit for anyone who needs me. Comfort all of us, Lord, with Your merciful presence in those things that grieve our hearts and minds.

Amen.

Shape My Heart with Love

There are six things the LORD hates, seven that are detestable to him: haughty eyes, a lying tongue, hands that shed innocent blood, a heart that devises wicked schemes, feet that are quick to rush into evil, a false witness who pours out lies and a person who stirs up conflict in the community.

PROVERBS 6:16–19 NIV

Heavenly Father,

I suspect the list from Proverbs is a lot shorter than it could be. Anything we do with a motive that is without love causes You pain. Anything we do that causes emotional or physical or spiritual harm to someone else grieves Your heart.

Help me to desire to be more like You, to be willing to be shaped with the wisdom that only love for others can bring. Help me to choose only those actions that benefit those around me. Let my words be kind, and let my spirit bring peace wherever I may go.

Keep me from even the slightest kind of arrogance so that I never dismiss another by a word or a look or an action. Help me to always be honest and giving, genuinely caring about the people in my sphere of influence. Please chase evil away from me and those I love. Help me to have a Samaritan's compassion and heart anyplace I go.

Amen.

Draw Near to God!

. . . .

Come near to God and he will come near to you. Wash your
hands, you sinners, and purify your hearts, you double-minded.
JAMES 4:8 NIV

Dear Lord,

When I say my good-night prayers, I can hardly wait to talk with You again in the morning. Then the alarm goes off before the last star has left the sky, and within moments of my feet hitting the floor, I'm up and running. Somewhere about halfway through the day, I realize that I've jumped into my routine and I flew out the door without You. I forgot step one. I forgot to seek Your face.

I'm sorry when I abandon the opportunity to share my heart with You in ways that bring me a clear perspective. Only with Your counsel can I get the vision for each thing I do, so that I am made clean in my thoughts, words, and actions by Your steadfast grace and love.

Lord, forgive me when I act in ways that are double-minded. Help me to surrender all I am to You, waiting for Your guidance before I even take a step. Cleanse me and wash me clean of those things that get in the way of our relationship. Help me start with a heart lovingly focused on You as I begin each day.

Amen.

A Noble and Good Heart

*"But the seed on good soil stands for those with a
noble and good heart, who hear the word, retain it,
and by persevering produce a crop."*

LUKE 8:15 NIV

Father God,

Thank You for providing plenty of good soil for new possibility in the lives of Your children. You inspire our work, bless us with hopes and dreams, and increase our understanding of life and all that we can become with Your help. When we seek Your direction, we grow strong and persevere to produce the fruit of our labors.

Help us when we neglect to plant Your seeds of possibility in good soil. Help us to understand what we need to do to keep going, even when it looks like we may get choked by weeds or when others try to discourage us from growing. Only You know exactly what we need to do to prepare the soil so we're ready to plant with each new opportunity. Only You can help us cultivate a better prayer life or a stronger faith to be on holy ground.

I ask that You would take the seed that is my heart and plant it firmly in Your Word; retain what is best about the work I do for You, and cause me to persevere in prayer and in my efforts to share Your love. Only then will I be able to produce a crop that will make us both proud. I seek Your favor on all that I am and all that I can be for Your kingdom.

Amen.

Your Heart's Desire

*May he give you the desire of your
heart and make all your plans succeed.*

PSALM 20:4 NIV

Dear Lord,

Ever since I was a kid, I've been wishing and hoping and praying for the good things in life for myself and for those around me. As I've matured in faith, I've understood that my greatest desire is to align my heart with Yours, my will with Your will for me. I know that when I give You all my hopes and dreams, You hand them back to me with the blessing that brings them to fruition. Oh, they may not be exactly what I thought I hoped or prayed for, or they may not be everything I even thought I would desire, but when I look at them in hindsight, I realize You have given me the better things. You have given me the real desires of my heart and helped me to succeed.

Today I pray for all who seek Your guidance about the future. I pray for those who come to You in prayer and believe with all their heart that the path of their desire is correct. I pray that You will show up for them and lead them to the places where they can serve You best.

I believe our deepest desires are to please You and do what we can to bless those around us. Help us as we make plans to always seek Your help in determining the steps we need to take. Help us to fulfill Your will and purpose for our lives.

Amen.

You Know When My Heart Hurts

You have turned for me my mourning into dancing; You have put off my sackcloth and clothed me with gladness, to the end that my glory may sing praise to You and not be silent. O LORD my God, I will give thanks to You forever.

PSALM 30:11–12 NKJV

Heavenly Father,

My heart is weighed down, broken and deeply grieved. I can hardly bear the sorrow that I feel. It is a lonely feeling. It is an abandoned, childlike, fearful feeling. It is a feeling of utter helplessness, for there is nothing that can change the circumstances, nothing that can heal the utter hurt.

I pray today that those feelings will pass in time and be replaced by the understanding that You have not left my side or abandoned me or neglected my sincerest heartfelt prayers. I know that in truth, You grieve with me when my heart is in pain, when my life goes into a pit of despair.

Lord, I ask that You would be with each person today who feels this kind of sorrow, who suffers from a broken heart. I ask that Your presence would be felt by them in ways they may never have experienced before. I ask that You comfort them with the kind of love only You can give and wait with them through the sadness and the sense of loss they feel.

Lord, thank You for being with us in the darkest moments of our lives, holding us gently and lovingly in Your tender hands.

Amen.

I'm a New Me Today

*Because of the LORD's great love we are not consumed,
for his compassions never fail. They are new every
morning; great is your faithfulness. I say to myself,
"The LORD is my portion; therefore I will wait for him."*

LAMENTATIONS 3:22–24 NIV

Dear Lord,

Some days it feels like the world just chews us up and spits us out. We aren't sure if we have the strength or the stamina to succeed at even the most menial tasks. We wonder if You still see us and if You know what we're going through.

We wait! Today I pray for all those who wait for You and who long for a glimpse of Your face or a chance to feel Your presence. I pray for those who seek relief from illness or financial stress or worry of any kind. I pray that Your light will shine upon them.

When I wait for You, Lord, it doesn't take long for me to realize You are near. In fact, in no time at all, I am renewed and refreshed in Your grace and mercy. I may not know the answers to my concerns, but I know You do and that You will help me see the direction to take.

Thank You for being so faithful to me. Help me to wait for You with patient hope, believing and trusting that You are indeed working things out and that the dark times will pass. I know the morning light will come again filled with Your love. You are my portion, and my heart waits for You with peace today.

Amen.

When Hope Is Gone

"Our time on earth is like a shadow. There is no hope."
1 Chronicles 29:15 NCV

Father in heaven,

The headlines are full of things that make my heart skip a beat. My heart races with fear and anxiety over all that is happening in the world. It seems that every news story is filled with violence and sadness and selfishness and greed. These are the very materials that create blindness and hearts of stone.

Lord, I know that time for any of us is short; in fact, it melts like the morning dew, evaporating like disappearing ink. I pray for all of us who seek You, who look to You with eyes of hope, and who long for Your hand to prevail and show us Your presence again.

Help all of us to move out of the shadows and into the light so that we may be a source of strength and love to those around us. Use me and others who call Your name to serve as a beacon of hope to those who are without hope at this very moment. You are the hope of the world, and all we can do is try to share Your hope with others.

I pray that those who are afraid or lonely or concerned about the heartbreaking things in this world would soften their hearts toward You and open the eyes of their hearts to see Your light.

Amen.

Forgiving Yourself and Others

. . . .

"Forget about the wrong things people do to you,
and do not try to get even. Love your neighbor
as you love yourself. I am the LORD."

LEVITICUS 19:18 NCV

Dear Lord,

You know me so well. You know that when someone hurts me, I struggle with how to make things right or how to be truly forgiving and not just give lip service to the idea of forgiveness. Sometimes I think I am forgiving someone as You would have me do, only to realize that the next time I encounter that person, I still remember the offense. I have not been able to forget.

I ask that You would help me be as forgiving to others as You are forgiving to me. You offer me forgiveness and then move my offense away from You as far as the east is from the west. You don't remember my sins after You've forgiven them. You take me back and hold me up and love me just as though I was brand-new, wiped clean of doing anything wrong.

Help me to be like that. Help me to be a person who does not remember offenses and who does not hold grudges. Only You know what motivates the hearts of others, and only You know my heart as well. Remind all of us to love others the way we are intended to love ourselves. Remind us also to forgive ourselves the way we would forgive others. Thank You for what You're doing, even now, to transform the way I perceive those who have offended me.

Amen.

Secrets of the Lord

*There are some things the LORD our God has kept
secret, but there are some things he has let us know.
These things belong to us and our children forever
so that we will do everything in these teachings.*

DEUTERONOMY 29:29 NCV

Dear Father and Teacher,

Thank You for sharing the things with me that You know I can handle. Thank You for revealing Yourself slowly, a little at a time, so that I can take in each lesson and learn how to live in ways that are holy. Thank You for teaching me the significance of my every thought, action, and deed.

I pray that Your wisdom and Your presence will be set firmly in the soul of each person who hungers for more of You. I pray that they would continually seek Your face and come to You when they have questions they simply don't know how to answer. Help each of us to step back from the world and step up to Your throne when we need help and nourishment and Your power and strength to live in the world.

Lord, we all desperately need You. We don't know all Your secrets, and we lack knowledge and spiritual insight. Help us to be willing to learn from You so that we can guide our children after us and help them come to know You.

Shape our hearts to want to know more of Your secrets. Help all Your children to discover Your ways and to inherit the blessing of Your salvation. Keep revealing all that we need to know as we come to You in prayer and seek You in Your Word. I ask for these things in the name of Jesus.

Amen.

Falling Down and Getting Up

- -

*For a righteous man may fall seven times and
rise again, but the wicked shall fall by calamity.*
PROVERBS 24:16 NKJV

Dear Lord,

I seem to be good at falling. By now I've fallen a lot more
than seven times. The amazing thing is that each time I slip and
fall, You help me to rise again. Each time I make a mess of things,
You come back and remind me who I am and what I might do to
change things for the better.

As many times as we've been through that process, You would
think I would get it, that I wouldn't have to learn this *falling and
rising* lesson over again. You would think I would just stay so close
to You that nothing could come between us and that I would only
walk in the ways You would have me go.

Lord, I'm disappointed with myself when I keep doing things
that I know are not good for me to do—actions that are not
strengthening my spirit or enriching my life. I'm sorry, and I pray
You will not give up on me in this process of aligning my heart
with Yours. I want to be more like You and less like me. Help me
and all of us who truly want to be more holy to follow You with an
expectant and loving heart, ready to rise to any occasion where
we are called for the sake of Your name.

Amen.

What's in a Name?

And God said to Moses, "I AM WHO I AM."
And He said, "Thus you shall say to the children
of Israel, 'I AM has sent me to you.'"

<small>EXODUS 3:14 NKJV</small>

Dear Creator God,

You have taught us that there is honor in a good name. You even changed the names of some of Your servants we know from the Bible to help them see that Your Spirit was intimately woven with theirs and that they were being called to do Your work. Sometimes I forget that You are on a first-name basis with all of us. You know exactly who we are and what we are.

Lord, I ask that You would help all of us remember how important Your name is to us so that we may never use Your name in vain or grieve Your Spirit. You have named us, chosen us, and given us a whole new identity. We are no longer our old selves but are made new by Your name and by the one name under heaven by which we may be saved, our Lord Jesus Christ.

Thank You for calling each one of us by name and helping us to get to know You better all the time. Help us to understand more of what it means to be a member of Your family each day. And Lord, let each of us say, "I AM has sent me," as we help to further the work of Your kingdom.

Amen.

Today's Headlines

GOD is my strength, GOD is my song, and, yes! GOD is my salvation. This is the kind of God I have and I'm telling the world! This is the God of my father—I'm spreading the news far and wide!

EXODUS 15:2 MSG

Dear Father God,

I am spreading the news! I will talk about You nonstop and share Your presence and Your Spirit and Your love with anybody who will listen. Help me to be brave enough to do that with great passion and compassion wherever I am, not concerning myself with how it might be received but trusting that You have guided me to speak.

We need You, Lord, and we need to share Your love for us because there are still so many people who do not know You. It breaks my heart to know that darkness covers the planet and yet light is readily available. We have been so stubborn, so unwilling to turn our faces to Your light, and because of that we cannot see the light in each other's faces. We cannot see what You are doing in our lives.

Help all of us who follow You to be about the business of spreading the news of Your love and faithfulness by either word or example, or a willingness to simply love others. I pray for the wisdom and the desire to tell the world that You are my strength, my song, and my salvation.

Amen.

Understanding Your Grace

But he said to me, "My grace is enough for you. When you are weak, my power is made perfect in you." So I am very happy to brag about my weaknesses. Then Christ's power can live in me.

2 CORINTHIANS 12:9 NCV

Dear Lord,

You have shown us that we live in grace, that we truly only exist in our present circumstances because You have allowed us to do so. We walk in grace and breathe it in like air, yet we don't truly recognize it or honor it. Our hearts should be overwhelmed with the awe of knowing Your grace sustains us and strengthens us and gives power to our lives. Your grace is enough, but only when we acknowledge that we simply can't live without it.

I pray for everyone who breathes in Your Spirit and walks in Your grace. I pray that they would praise You with song and tell others of Your goodness. I pray that they would know that You are the power behind anything they do that helps to build the kingdom and that You alone have given them the strength to love others in the ways that make a difference. Whatever we can do for good, Lord, I pray that we would do it today filled with Your Spirit and Your grace, strengthened with the kind of power that excites our hearts and keeps us moving forward.

Shape us even more so that we plug into Your power for our lives. Thank You for extending Your amazing grace to us each day.

Amen.

When Your Heart Is Not in It!

*Therefore we do not lose heart. Though outwardly we are
wasting away, yet inwardly we are being renewed day by day.*

2 CORINTHIANS 4:16 NIV

Dear Lord,

Some days I feel like a waste of space. My heart is simply not
into the things I know You want me to do. Whether it's simple stuff
like helping my neighbor or something more difficult like leading
a Bible study, I'm just out of sorts.

Today, I pray for all of us who lose heart or feel overwhelmed
and uncertain. Help us to renew our minds by reading Your Word
and to refresh our spirits by listening to You and talking to You in
prayer. Help us to see Your hand at work in our lives in a way we
may not have noticed before. Remind us of who we are and all that
You are doing each day to keep us strong.

Open our hearts to each other so that fresh breezes of love
blow in and keep us feeling alive and energized and ready to serve
You. Forgive me when my heart is at a temporary standstill, especially when I'm needed to help someone else get closer to You.

Let me always be a person with a willing heart. . .willing to
serve You and the people around me in ways that show Your heart
for the world.

Amen.

When My Heart Is Happy

You who are young, be happy while you are young,
and let your heart give you joy in the days of your youth.

ECCLESIASTES 11:9 NIV

Dear God,

Today, I just want to thank You for giving me a happy heart. Though we are reminded to be happy while we are young, I believe that You have given us ageless hearts, capable of true happiness at any time in life when we choose to remember all You've done for us and all You've given us.

It's funny to realize that when we're truly young and imagine we'll live forever, we take our days for granted and think we have endless tomorrows in which to be happy. Then, as we grow older and a bit more aware of the patterns of life, we realize we must choose the gift of happiness for ourselves. We must decide that we have many reasons to count our blessings and that each of those blessings exists simply because You sustain us and want us to be joyful.

I pray we will recognize the gifts of each day and that with youthful zeal, whatever our age, we will be happy in heart and in spirit. We will be happy because of all You've done to give us the things that matter in this life. Bless those who seek Your face with peace and abundance, with joy beyond measure. Father, today I choose joy because You have given me grace and mercy and peace and endless reasons to smile. Keep me young at heart no matter what age I may happen to be.

Amen.

When I Talk about God

. . . .

*Then everyone will fear God. They will tell what God
has done, and they will learn from what he has done.*
PSALM 64:9 NCV

Dear Lord,

Oh, how I pray to learn from Your loving example. Grant me
the heart of a student as I strive to learn from Your Word. Grant
me wisdom as I seek to define Your purpose for the things I do.
Help me to learn from those around me who love me and who
pray for my good.

Encourage me to share the stories You've given me and to brag
of Your goodness and Your faithfulness so that I might influence how
others think and how they live, drawing them closer to Your side.

I am not able to make a list of all You've done and all You will
do to give me vision and knowledge and awareness and passion
for life. Whatever I might note would only present more memories
of Your protection or Your grace when we least expect it. We so
easily lose sight of the grace we received yesterday when we
struggle with some difficulty in the present. Most of the time we
aren't very far away from being just like those grumbling children
of Israel who could literally see Your presence every day in the
pillar of fire and in the cloud.

Lord, help me to point the way to You and to do it proudly
and boldly wherever I may be. You are the light of my life and the
joy of my heart.

Amen.

Praying for Your Favor

*And since it is through God's kindness, then it is not
by their good works. For in that case, God's grace
would not be what it really is—free and undeserved.*

ROMANS 11:6 NLT

Dear Lord,

When my heart is full or when it feels overwhelmed by my current circumstances, I find myself praying, even wishing and hoping, for Your favor. I believe in Your kindness to me, and I trust that You will prevail and that Your plans for me will succeed.

I say this, though, knowing that I cannot earn Your favor. You give me Your favor because of Your amazing grace and Your willingness to help me. You give me favor that is free and undeserved. You want my life to be good, and You want to draw me closer to You.

Thank You for Your free gift of grace. Thank You for the favor You show me and everyone else simply because we have accepted and embraced Jesus, and because Your love for Him is the same love that lives within us now.

Help each of us to show favor to others any chance we get, because all of us need Your help and we do not exist alone. We come before You with thanks and praise.

Amen.

Give Me Eyes to See

*Then everyone who has eyes will be able to see the truth,
and everyone who has ears will be able to hear it.*

Isaiah 32:3 NLT

Dear God,

We live in a world where it is sometimes difficult to define the truth. We think it is politically correct to allow each person to live by the truth as they see it. Conflict exists in our hearts, though, because when we give each other room to be the person You designed us to be, we feel uncertain and must face our own sense of bias, our own assumptions of what we imagine someone else should be.

What we perceive may or may not be truth. . .that is, divine truth. We can only receive such truth from the one source that is never going to change; we can only receive truth from You. Help us to hear Your truth with spiritual ears, and let us see truth with a spiritual heart.

We know that divine truth is very different from human truth and that Your ways are not our ways. We know that when we draw near to You, we have a much clearer understanding of our personal circumstances. It is by divine truth that we have come to understand that You alone are the source of all we know to be love. You are the reason we are so desperate to find You and to live in that love. Open our eyes to Your truth and our ears to perceive all that You want us to know. Thank You for giving us the ultimate truth, Your Son, Jesus.

Amen.

What Time Is It?

He has made everything beautiful in its time. Also He has put eternity in their hearts, except that no one can find out the work that God does from beginning to end.

ECCLESIASTES 3:11 NKJV

Dear Lord,

You have put eternity in our hearts because You let us know that even though our time on earth comes to an end, our time with You can be forever. Help those who are uncertain about Your eternal love so that they can begin to live with You right now. Soften their hearts in ways that cause them to desire to learn more of You so that they can recognize Your voice as You seek to guide them.

We have so little time on earth to get to know You, or even to get to know ourselves. Bless us with exactly the amount of time we need to decide to be with You for all eternity. I pray for all the people on this earth who don't yet know You, that You would provide a way for them to draw near to You. I pray that their good hearts and their lives would be in Your hand.

Lord, You made everything beautiful, and when we have hearts that perceive You, the things in life fill us with joy and define our happiness. Help us to grasp enough of Your divine intentions for us that we may be shaped and molded to live for Your glory. Make each of us beautiful in Your time and in Your Spirit.

Amen.

Another Birthday

. . . .

He asked you for life, and you gave it to him, so his years
go on and on. He has great glory because you gave
him victories; you gave him honor and praise.

PSALM 21:4–5 NCV

Dear heavenly Father,

I know that the psalmist is referring to himself as King David, the one who asked You for life and You gave him even more besides. However, I sense the prayer is not only his but mine as well. I ask You for life that I may live in a way that pleases You. I ask You for life that I might have victories in my work and in my relationships with others. I ask You for life so that each birthday would have meaning and I could understand more clearly the very purpose for which I exist.

Long ago, I asked You for life, and You gave me more than I ever imagined to be possible. You gave me the gifts of family and friends and people to love. You gave me honor and victory in the things I can accomplish and in the work I do. You have more than provided for me by continually blessing the work of my hands.

Thank You for being the author of my life. Each time a birthday comes, I celebrate You and the joys that I have because of all You've given me. I give You honor and praise, for I am blessed beyond measure. You are the one who lights my way with joy.

Amen.

Fashion My Heart

. . . .

Create in me a clean heart, O God,
and renew a steadfast spirit within me.

PSALM 51:10 NKJV

Dear God of my heart,

I am so in need of Your divine touch today. I need to know that You hold me in Your gentle hand, sculpting me, shaping me, causing me to have a heart like Yours so I can share that heart with others. I need to know that I can honor You with the things I do and that any success that comes to me is because of Your grace and mercy.

Help me and others who walk with You to desire more of Your heart, to want to be more like You in every possible way. Help us to surrender the stony parts of our hearts so that You can keep teaching and guiding us to be better people.

I know that without Your help, my spirit would suffer and become parched and dry. So today, I pray for a refreshed and renewed sense of Your presence so that I can be the best possible me and serve You in every way possible. You are my strength and my rock. Grant me a clean heart, and let my spirit rejoice in You.

Amen.

Nothing but Today

. . . .

Grace teaches us to live in the present age in a wise and right way and in a way that shows we serve God. We should live like that while we wait for our great hope and the coming of the glory of our great God and Savior Jesus Christ.

TITUS 2:12–13 NCV

Dear Lord,

I know that sometimes we forget the very air we breathe is a blessing, and each day when we rise it is because You have called us back to life. We can take for granted the hours in a day or the opportunities that come to us, never once thanking You for making everything possible. Without You, we are nothing. Without Your grace to give us wisdom and guidance, we would surely not serve You well.

As we go about our business today, let us remember that this day is all we truly have. This moment is ours, and we are not guaranteed anything more. When we think like that, we use our time and our talents wisely. We spend our hours with greater desire to know You better and greater hope to live in joy.

I pray that all Your children would embrace the present moment, seeking Your face in all they do. Help each of us live with expectation and intention, knowing that each moment is critical to all we are meant to be. Help all of us serve You with a wholehearted desire to do what we can to make each moment count.

Amen.

Walking with God

And what does the LORD require of you but to do justly,
to love mercy, and to walk humbly with your God?
MICAH 6:8 NKJV

Dear God,

When I was a kid, I used to wear saddle shoes. I didn't like them. I thought other kids would think I was too poor to have pretty shoes. Those saddle shoes made me walk funny and made me feel funny, too.

Now that I can pick any type of shoe I want to wear, I realize that my shoes aren't what matter in the grand scheme of things. In fact, if I walk barefoot, that would be okay, too.

What's important is that I have a big desire to walk in Your shoes, Lord. I can put on whatever shoes I want to wear for the day and follow You in every way. I may have shoes that pinch my toes, or shoes that take me right out of my comfort zone, but if I'm intent on fitting my life into Your way of living, then I can walk with You all the time. You just want me to walk humbly by Your side.

I pray for all of us who want to walk with You more closely, who understand that we can put on our humble saddle shoes and do the work You've called us to do with love and mercy; and when we do, we'll be dazzling. We'll be a dazzling light for Your love. Thanks for walking with me today. Thank You that I can have happy feet, no matter what shoes I wear. . .as long as I am on Your path and following You.

Amen.

Forgive Me Again

Dear Lord,

It's taken time for me to understand and appreciate the power of forgiveness, especially Your forgiveness. I don't think I have always been clear about the importance of what happens when we forgive others or when someone forgives us.

I have even taken Your forgiveness for granted. I have given lip service to You, not always understanding the gravity of my requests to forgive others or to be forgiven by You. Today I want to change that. I want to give You unending thanks and praise for Your willingness to continually forgive the things I do that grieve Your heart. I want to seek Your guidance and ask for a right spirit within me to do the things that please You.

I understand now that only through forgiveness can a slate become clean, a heart changed, or a life encouraged to move forward. Forgiveness makes us new in You, and it causes us to want to do better. Lord, I pray for everyone who seeks Your forgiveness, and I pray that each of us will be anointed with Your Holy Spirit in ways that will lift us up and make us value doing the right thing. I thank You that Your mercy endures forever.

Amen.

My Brothers and Sisters

*Therefore, my brothers and sisters, make every effort to confirm
your calling and election. For if you do these things, you will
never stumble, and you will receive a rich welcome into the
eternal kingdom of our Lord and Savior Jesus Christ.*

2 PETER 1:10–11 NIV

Dear Lord,

Thank You for giving us brothers and sisters. For many of us,
these are the people who are the dearest to our hearts, the ones
who see us as we are and love us just the same. Brothers and sisters are a unique part of a family because siblings learn to grow
up together, experience a lot of the same things in life, and figure
out how to interpret the world at large.

Even if we have no biological siblings, You have given us
many brothers and sisters in Christ. You have blessed us beyond
measure with people who are there for us, eager to help us learn
and grow. You have helped us experience life in ways that give us
a desire to reach out and share what we know, give what we can
give in times of need, and shine a light when darkness overtakes us.

Lord, today I pray for brothers and sisters everywhere, the
biological ones, the spiritual ones, and even the adopted ones.
These are the members of our families who make a difference and
help us to grow and become more than we could ever become
alone. These are the people who support our dreams and shape
our tomorrows. I thank You for my own sisters and brothers with
all my heart.

Amen.

Family Heirlooms

In his great mercy he has given us new birth into a living hope through the resurrection of Jesus Christ from the dead, and into an inheritance that can never perish, spoil or fade. This inheritance is kept in heaven for you, who through faith are shielded by God's power.

1 PETER 1:3–5 NIV

Father God,

Sometimes I don't give enough thought to what it means to be Your child. I love that You know my name and that You have already prepared a place for me in heaven. I love that, but then I ask myself what I am doing to pass along the blessing. How can I give my family the kind of heirlooms that will never perish or spoil or fade?

We live in trying times, and we live in a world where everything is disposable. The things that were precious to our ancestors are often long forgotten, replaced by the newest gadgets of the moment. The problem is that none of these new gadgets will last or bring us joy for eternity. Help us not only to share our faith with others but to live our short lives as redeemed people who serve as an example to those around us. Help us provide our children the one gift of inheritance that matters. . .the way to Your door.

Hear our prayers today for all Your children, especially those who do not yet understand the joy that can be theirs right now because of what You have already done for us. You have given us an incredible heritage that will keep us close to You forever. Thank You for Your gracious gift.

Amen.

Having It My Way

Show me how you work, GOD;
school me in your ways.

PSALM 25:4 MSG

Lord,

Why is it that I get lost and confused and unhappy anytime I try too hard to have everything my way? I don't usually think of myself as stubborn, but that may be a fair way to describe my attitude. When I look at my desire to have things my way with my mind, I can give myself all kinds of reasons to think my actions are acceptable. I can even imagine that I am in control.

But then, when I look at this question of attitude with my heart, everything becomes clear. It becomes clear to me that I have not been willing to surrender my life completely to You. I recognize those areas where I am desperately trying to maintain control and I wonder why. Can I do a better job than You would do with the details of my life? I don't think so. Do I know what is up ahead so that I can determine my steps in a way that will provide for my well-being and my greatest possibility?

Lord, please forgive me when I get in the way of Your work. I raise my hands and my heart to You today and relinquish all that I want to accomplish, all that I hope and dream, knowing full well that every aspect of my life is safer in Your hands than mine. Thank You for watching over me with such great love.

Amen.

A Cup of Wisdom

But if any of you needs wisdom, you should ask
God for it. He is generous to everyone and will
give you wisdom without criticizing you.

JAMES 1:5 NCV

Dear Lord,

English writer and philosopher William Hazlitt once wrote that those who have the largest hearts have the soundest understanding. I like the idea of that, even if I'm not sure of its validity. I certainly pray to have a "large" heart in the sense that I am seeking to continually grow in my understanding of You and of all that You would have me be in this world.

I know that I need Your faithful companionship to help me be aligned with Your intentions for me. Help all of us to seek Your face when we need to make wise choices or when we struggle with something we simply can't understand. Help us to lean in and listen for Your voice, knowing that we cannot move forward without You.

If having a large heart means that we have a certainty and a clarity of what it means to have Your love each day, then help all of us to desire hearts that grow in wisdom and love for others. Help us to want to know You better so that we see Your hand at work in the things we do. Grant that we would have no fear in coming to Your throne when we don't understand what to do next. You alone have our lives in Your hand, and we are Yours, heart and mind and soul. Thank You for hearing our prayers and helping us to be wise.

Amen.

Step by Step

When people's steps follow the LORD, God is pleased with their ways. If they stumble, they will not fall, because the LORD holds their hand.

PSALM 37:23–24 NCV

Heavenly Father,

The steps are not always even, and the path can be rocky. It doesn't feel certain or easy to discover the most direct route. It is troublesome and causes a delay. It brings my heart a taste of misery. This is how I feel, Lord, every time I walk away from You.

I don't know what causes me to take the path You would not choose for me, the one that is more difficult to walk because I have to walk it alone. Each time I take some other path and look back to where I wanted to go, I realize there is one gaping problem. I chose to stop following You and just walk on ahead, thinking I could find the way all by myself. It fills my heart with sorrow every time I start to wander from Your side. I don't even realize I've done it until I get far enough away that I literally find myself looking up again to see if You are near. It's troubling, and I know You do not want me to walk the path alone.

Lord, I know that You love me and Your hope is for me to follow You each day. You did not set me on the long, winding path that leads to the wilderness. Forgive me when I walk off without You. Help me to hold on to Your hand and stay close to Your side today.

Amen.

Prodigal Me

" 'I will leave and return to my father and say to him, "Father, I have sinned against God and against you. I am no longer worthy to be called your son, but let me be like one of your servants.' " So the son left and went to his father. While the son was still a long way off, his father saw him and felt sorry for his son. So the father ran to him and hugged and kissed him."

LUKE 15:18–20 NCV

Dear Father,

How often I stray from You. Most of the time, it's not even intentional. I imagine that I'm on a firm foundation, that I've said my prayers and surrendered the day to You, only to discover that I simply drifted from Your side. Sometimes I drift away with the news. I try to discover the latest worldview of how to live, how to give, and how to react to the culture I live in. The more my mind tries to stretch and bend to meet the current standards, the less I truly see Your face.

I know that I have only one choice. I cannot always find You with head knowledge or with an eye to letting those around me live however it pleases them. I can't always discern the options and possibilities, and I know that Your ways are not my ways. Lord, I pray to seek You with my heart. I pray that my heart will hope and trust and desire more of You. I pray that all those who look for You today will find You, willingly surrendering their hearts so that they can come back to You in peace.

Wrap Your arms around us and keep us safe from the world's conflicts and deceptions. Let us come home to You every time we seek Your face.

Amen.

Financial Woes

*"Seek first God's kingdom and what God wants.
Then all your other needs will be met as well."*

MATTHEW 6:33 NCV

Dear Lord,

Thank You for all You do each day to provide for my needs. I know that I sometimes worry about my financial position and wonder whether I'll have enough money each month to take care of all the bills. It seems like I always have more bills than money, and it feels like a cycle that has been going on for a long time.

Forgive me when I spend more time than I should looking at the bills and the obstacles to getting my finances straight than I do on simply trusting in Your provision. When I look at things with my mind, I don't see You clearly. I always hope and pray that by some miracle, I'll have what I need, but I wrestle with the doubt of whether that will be so.

Lord, I realize that there are a lot of people who pray for the miracle of Your provision; and when I think about the ways You take care of me, I know that my life and my finances are securely in Your hand. You have shown up so many times and in so many ways to help me, and I thank You for that. Help me to be more grateful for what I have and more willing to leave my financial woes at Your feet. Bless me and Your people everywhere who call on Your name. Provide all of them with their daily bread, and grant them peace and contentment in all things.

Amen.

Embarrassed

· ·

I prayed, "My God, I am too ashamed and embarrassed to lift up my face to you, my God, because our sins are so many. They are higher than our heads. Our guilt even reaches up to the sky."

EZRA 9:6 NCV

Dear Father,

I once read a quote from Mark Twain that said, "Man is the only animal that blushes. Or needs to." I'm blushing today, embarrassed to come before You and confess the things I've done lately that grieve Your Spirit. I sometimes let the little sins pass by as though I don't notice them. The problem is that I'm usually very aware of my little sins of omission or commission. I know when I've done something wrong, and it saddens me that I don't have the strength of character or even the desire to be better.

Forgive me when I embarrass both of us by my behavior. Help me not only to do better but to desire with all my heart to align my thoughts and actions with Your will for me. Help me to seek to be more like You, and give me a clean heart, full of joy in You and ready to do only those things You would ask of me.

Bless everyone today who may be somewhat embarrassed about a past behavior or a sin, no matter how great or small it may be. Give us hearts like Yours to share with everyone we know.

Amen.

Who Is On First?

The silence was deafening—they had been arguing with one another over who among them was greatest. He sat down and summoned the Twelve. "So you want first place? Then take the last place. Be the servant of all."

MARK 9:34–35 MSG

Dear Lord,

What is it that makes us think we are entitled to the best seat in the house? Some of us are leaders or speakers or educators, and we imagine those things give us priority, or a front-row seat. Some of us are politicians or theologians or philosophers, and we think we've earned the right to be in the box seats of life. Unfortunately, even if we have some claim to fame, we don't stay there, and then we suffer disappointment or even anger.

Forgive us when we think we deserve more than others, when we imagine You favor us over the rest of the people in the crowd. You have been trying to teach us since the days of the disciples that those on first are really servants of each other, giving and sharing all that they have so everyone can thrive.

Help us to keep You on first today. When You are first, we know that other things will come together for our good and that it won't matter what seat we have in any arena because we'll be seated next to You and sharing in Your joy. Give us hearts to seek You first so that we can serve others better.

Amen.

Can We Trust God to Answer Our Prayers?

God answered their prayers because they trusted him.
1 CHRONICLES 5:20 MSG

Dear Father,

We spend a good share of our lives learning what it means to trust others. As children, we trust our parents because they are the ones who protect us and give us food and shelter. We go to school and begin to trust teachers and other adults and to develop trust in relationships with friends and teammates. Finally, we move into the world, and we learn to trust coworkers to be dependable and accountable. We also learn to trust that love is real and that people keep their promises.

The problem for many of us, even from the beginning, even from the first trust relationships with parents or teachers or friends, was that things fell apart quickly and we were left wondering what trust was all about. As we grew to be adults and learned more and more that few people kept their word, the concept of trust simply melted away until we finally realized we couldn't even trust ourselves.

My prayer today, God, is that You would give each of us a trusting heart so we would learn all over again to trust others. Open our hearts so we recognize that the one thing, the one source for all trust comes from You. Help us understand that we can trust You with all that we are and all we hope to be. Grant that we might trust Your love for us with each new sunrise. Give us hearts that trust in You for every prayer we speak.

Amen.

Show Me the Way

*Trust the LORD with all your heart, and don't depend
on your own understanding. Remember the LORD
in all you do, and he will give you success.*
PROVERBS 3:5–6 NCV

Father in heaven,

Whatever I do today, help me to seek Your guidance before I take a step in any direction. Help me to recognize that even if I think I know which way to go and what to do, things will come out better if I ask for Your help before I begin. You know the details. You know what each choice I make involves and who might be affected and what changes need to happen. Help me to lean on You for the sake of everyone around me. When I walk with You, I serve others better, and that gives me strength and confidence.

When I walk off without You, please nudge my heart and remind me that we need to go together. When I imagine I have all the answers, help me to check in with You to see if there is anything I've missed or if there is some other step to take that will serve You better. We pride ourselves on our independence and our own abilities to handle life's circumstances, but I know that anything I do that is independent of You has no measure of success built in. Help me to trust You to work out in me the best things I can do in every conversation and every action I take today. Show me the way, Lord, and I will follow.

Amen.

Don't Give Up on Me

....

But, LORD, don't be far away.
You are my strength; hurry to help me.
PSALM 22:19 NCV

Dear Lord,

How many times have I run to You when I'm weary and life is spinning out of control? I know that You don't give up on me even when I've contributed to the uncertainty and the misery I'm feeling. I know that You're near even when I'm worrying and losing my sense of direction.

I pray for everyone who feels they've lost their strength. You once gave Samson a special kind of strength, one that was based on his obedience to You and his willingness to serve You as You requested. Sadly, he allowed his own strength to be taken from him simply because he grew weary of the circumstances around him. He grew tired of keeping a secret, and it cost him his life.

Fortunately, You've given us the kind of strength through Your Spirit that doesn't depend on keeping a secret. In fact, our strength is renewed in You when we share more of our faith and tell Your stories. Our strength grows as we remind ourselves of all You've done and how many times You've rescued us from those things that weigh us down. Lord, we need Your help every day. We need to know that You are close and that we cannot get too far away from You. Shape our hearts so that with every breath we seek Your direction, knowing that our strength and our lives are in Your hand. Thank You for never giving up on me.

Amen.

Why Is Everything a Mess?

The LORD is kind and does what is right; our God is merciful. The LORD watches over the foolish; when I was helpless, he saved me. I said to myself, "Relax, because the LORD takes care of you."

PSALM 116:5–7 NCV

Dear God,

Just when I think I've stopped doing the foolish things in this world, I discover that I've done it again; I've created chaos. Forgive me for getting myself into this craziness. I am here again asking You to help me clean up the mess.

Father, I realize that what I need is a change of heart and attitude. I need to give You every part of me so You can mold and shape me into the person You've called me to be, so that I can grow in my faith and my desire to serve You. So often, I let the mundane matters of life get in the way of the things I know I should do, and then I make foolish choices, or at best unconsidered choices.

I pray that You would help all of us who get ourselves in trouble simply because we do not surrender our lives or our days to You. Forgive our foolishness, and give us wisdom through Your Holy Spirit to do better next time. Grant that we could look to You first, take the steps that are healthy for our lives, and then relax in Your care and keeping. Thank You for Your mercy and grace. Help me once again to clean up the mess caused by my own folly.

Amen.

A Lesson in Light

. . . .

But even the darkness is not dark to you. The night is as light as the day; darkness and light are the same to you.

PSALM 139:12 NCV

Dear Lord,

Sometimes we feel overpowered by the darkness. We lose our way and stumble over the obstacles we cannot clearly see. We wonder if You are still with us and if You can see us right where we are. It brings us moments of fear and trembling. We are in such need of the light.

I pray for all of us who may feel that we are walking in the dark, unable to understand the circumstances of life, the chaos of the world. Help us to recognize and learn the lesson of Your light. Help us to remember it, memorize it, and bring it back to our minds anytime we need it. Grant us the awareness that You are never confused by darkness. You are never uncertain of the path before us because the darkness and the light are all the same to You. You created both to live side by side, perhaps to always remind us that You see clearly twenty-four hours a day, in the darkness or in the light.

Lord, whenever the darkness seems too confining, too scary, I pray that You will shine Your ever-present, steadfast beam in my direction. I pray that You will let Your face shine today on Your children who are stumbling around wondering where You are and if You know they are in need of You. You alone are the light of this world, and I pray that we may all stand close to Your light every day.

Amen

Obstacles Lesson

* *

But Jesus was matter-of-fact: "Yes—and if you embrace this
kingdom life and don't doubt God, you'll not only do minor feats
like I did to the fig tree, but also triumph over huge obstacles."

MATTHEW 21:21 MSG

Heavenly Father,

I embrace the kingdom life and do my best to draw closer to
You each day. It's a process that feels overwhelming sometimes and
very simple other times. Perhaps I'm not sure what it means to truly
"embrace the kingdom life." Perhaps I have not yet surrendered
enough of myself so You can continue to teach me in ways that
give me the courage to reach out to others in Your name.

I'm sure I couldn't walk up to a tree and cause it to wither simply
because I told it to, but I realize there's a bigger issue to consider.
I tend to look at the obstacles I put in the way of embracing You.
Yet, in my heart, I remain steadfast in my desire to serve You and
discover more about how to be like You.

From all that I know so far, I recognize that this transition in
me is a matter of the heart. I can only embrace the kingdom life
from a heart direction. Nothing else will work because daily life
continues to put obstacles in the path. I ask that You would help
me and others to stop looking around at the obstacles and to look
up at Your face. Help us to embrace You first so that we can be a
resource for good to others who seek You. Help us to trust that
we can do all You've called us to do because You are always with
us and we can triumph over the obstacles.

Amen.

Turn Me Around

Is there anyone around to save Israel?
Yes. GOD is around; GOD turns life around.
PSALM 14:7 MSG

Father in heaven,

Whew! What a ride life can be! When I think I know exactly where I'm headed and I lift my hands in the air and just hang on for the ride, there's suddenly a jolt of surprise and everything turns in a different direction. I wonder how it is that I can keep up with the way You want me to go when I suffer this kind of whiplash that doesn't even seem to be part of my own design.

Of course, when I reflect on this, I realize that there is nothing that surprises You. You always know my direction, and You know the obstacles that will present themselves. You even know how I will respond. Lord, I pray specifically today that You will help me to seek Your counsel on what to do when it's time to turn around. Help me to know whether I'm facing a simple obstacle that can be removed with prayer or whether I need to try again or do something completely new.

You know when it's time to move forward and when it's time to turn around. I'm grateful that You allow U-turns because You know my sense of direction is not very accurate. Help me and those who seek Your face to know when to move forward and when to look for a new direction or another open door. Knowing when to turn around can give us a lot of peace and save us a lot of heartache.

Amen.

Peace in My Soul

"I am the LORD your God, who teaches you what is best for you, who directs you in the way you should go. If only you had paid attention to my commands, your peace would have been like a river, your well-being like the waves of the sea."

ISAIAH 48:17–18 NIV

Lord God,

That peace like a river thing sounds so good. I can imagine a sleepy little river winding its way around the mountain paths, letting go of all its cares and woes and heading out to the seas, ready to splash and play. It's a beautiful picture, and I ask myself why it is that I don't listen to Your commands more closely so I can have that kind of peace. Why is it that I'm so intent on wandering around the world on my own, as if I actually knew what was best for me?

Lord, I want that peace You offer. I want the peace that flows like a river from my head to my toes, and I want that kind of peace for all the people I love. Help all of us to be more attentive to Your voice and to focus more carefully on the direction You would have us go. Grant that we would be able to spend more of our lives enjoying that kind of serenity and peace.

Bless each person today who is seeking Your direction, and give them peace like a river all day through.

Amen.

Where Are You When I Need You?

*"And surely I am with you always,
to the very end of the age."*

MATTHEW 28:20 NIV

Father in heaven,

I know in my heart that You are always with me. You're there when my day is going well, when I manage to achieve some sense of success, and when life is going along in a good way.

For some reason, when life is not going along in a good way, I find it more difficult to know if You're still beside me. I see the heartache of a friend, or I grieve the loss of someone I loved or of a dream that seemed important, and I wonder where You are. Do You see me when things are going haywire?

Of course, deep down I know the answer. I know that troubles come to all of us and that no one escapes the gains and losses of life. I pray for people everywhere who suffer from any kind of loss—physical, spiritual, emotional—and I ask that You bring Your grace and comfort and let them feel Your very real presence.

All of us need You, and there are never moments when it is best for us to be left alone. Help us to seek Your voice and Your embrace for all that will come today, and bless us with peace.

Amen.

Make No Mistake

. . . .

We all stumble in many ways. Anyone who is never at fault in
what they say is perfect, able to keep their whole body in check.

JAMES 3:2 NIV

Dear Lord,

Thank You for this new day and the chance to try again to be a good servant. Help me to get past any mistakes I made yesterday and to recognize that each morning brings a new opportunity to do better. Sometimes my mistakes are simple ones and can be easily fixed. Sometimes they carry more weight, and they grieve my heart to think of them. I pray for Your peace and Your forgiveness for those.

Bless all Your children who recognize the error of their ways and who strive to do better in the world. If they've fallen short of the mark You set for them, I pray that You would guide their steps and their thoughts. Give them wise counsel, and surround them with people who can shine a light on their best direction. You know each one of us and what motivates us. You know who we are and where we are weak. Examine our sins built on ego that keep us from doing a better job for You, and make us mindful of the need to change.

Sometimes the media plays up the troubles of the world so much that we wonder what good we can possibly do. We wonder if it's even worth it to strive for a better day and a new path. After all, everyone makes mistakes. Yet, Lord, we know that with You, we can all rise above our own humanity and seek something that is far more holy. Help us to desire that kind of holiness.

Amen.

What to Believe

. . . .

"If you believed Moses, you would believe me, for he wrote about me. But since you do not believe what he wrote, how are you going to believe what I say?"

JOHN 5:46–47 NIV

Dear Lord,

I miss the days when I was so innocent that I could simply believe that everything was possible and that good would prevail. I loved my small-town life experience as a child that brought neighbors together when someone needed a helping hand, or that brought the sound of church bells ringing when blessings were being shared in the community. Those were days when I knew what to believe and when I trusted in all the good things in life.

Sadly, my grown-up world is far more complex. Now there's so much information on the Internet or on other social networks that things get blurry, obscured by so many opinions, either thoughtful or ill-conceived. It becomes hard to know what to believe or who to believe.

One source of comfort for me, though, is to turn off the news and turn off the computer and head for my daily dose of scripture. Somehow when I come back to You for reassurance and a sense of calm, I find it every time, simply waiting quietly for me to notice. Thank You for being my guide and my opportunity to understand that I can trust You because in You I know what to believe.

Amen.

A Grown-Up Teaching

*So let us go on to grown-up teaching. Let us not go back
over the beginning lessons we learned about Christ.*

HEBREWS 6:1 NCV

Dear Father,

You called to me back when I was a child, and I understood that You loved me right there, just as I was. You nurtured me and helped me grow up to know more about You. I've stumbled and fallen many times in that process, but You've always helped me get back on my feet and shown me once again what to do.

Now that I'm a grown-up and You're feeding me more than the milk You once gave me, I realize that human beings have serious choices to make—serious and blessed. You know who and what we are. You know the path You want us to pursue to achieve the purposes for which we were born. Help us to receive You into our lives with the same love and passion and desire that we had as children. Help us to trust You with everything we have so that the world does not try to steal us away from Your presence. Cause us to be willing to grow and change and become Your true servants.

We all need a good teacher; and if we are willing to listen to Your voice and heed Your words, we'll know in our hearts how to move to the head of the class. Help all of us to be honor students for You and to be determined to grow stronger in Your name.

Amen.

Let Your Yes Be Yes!

The yes to all of God's promises is in Christ,
and through Christ we say yes to the glory of God.
2 CORINTHIANS 1:20 NCV

Dear Lord,

People are often not particularly careful about the promises they make. We say, "I'll get back to you about your concerns," and then we never take time to get back to the person in question. We say, "I'll be there for you," and yet for a lot of reasons, we're not available when we're needed. Or we do worse things: we say things we know we don't mean just to move past an uncomfortable situation. We overpromise and we underdeliver. We're all part of this equation one way or another, yet we are disturbed when someone lies to us.

Lord, I admit that I sometimes say things I don't really mean. I don't do it to be unkind, but more likely because I'm trying to be aware of someone else's feelings. Whether we genuinely recognize our own motives for not letting our "yes mean yes," please help us to be more careful about what we say and especially about things we promise. In particular, let us be honorable people.

You promise to be near us and to listen to our prayers and to love us and to take us back to heaven one day. Lord, I take those promises to heart, because I trust that Your yes means yes. Let my words and my promises be the kind I can live up to and deliver. Let my yes be trustworthy. Let my promises be made with my whole heart.

Amen.

Be Still My Heart!

*LORD, you are my hope. LORD,
I have trusted you since I was young.*
PSALM 71:5 NCV

Lord God,

Some days go by without me even noticing all You've done. I go about my business and do what I can, and with a prayerful nod in Your direction, I simply go to bed and start again the next day. My confession now, though, is that I recognize that in living my life that way, I may miss out on an opportunity or a blessing You have for me. I probably miss something incredible that You had done. You are always doing amazing things, and that's what gives hope to our hearts.

My personal failures do not deter You from doing good for me or for those I love. My neglect of spending quiet time with You, or not spending enough time in Your Word or in prayer, may not please You; but it still doesn't keep You from doing what You can to please me. Your love for me causes me to stop and reflect and rejoice in what You've given me. I can only say one thing: "Be still my heart!"

I realize that You are bigger than any situation I might find myself in, and You are stronger than any stubborn streak I display. You are the reason I can live in hope, because without You this world is lost and would feel even crazier than it does. You are the difference, and I want to thank You for giving Your only Son to this fallen planet. Thank You for being the hope of the world and for being so steadfast and trustworthy. I pray that I might be worthy of Your trust as well.

Amen.

It's a Heartless World

....

People did not think it was important to have a true knowledge of God. So God left them and allowed them to have their own worthless thinking and to do things they should not do. They are filled with every kind of sin, evil, selfishness, and hatred.

ROMANS 1:28–29 NCV

Dear Lord,

You draw near to us and do Your best to teach us how to live so that we can honor You and prosper in the world. You show us what it means to have compassionate hearts, and You deliver us from untold evils, holding on to us even when we look the other way.

We need You so much! We cannot truly survive without You in either this world or the next. We don't know how naive we are, and our only hope is to acknowledge Your holiness and seek to discover how we can be more like You, for without You we are walking on a high wire without a net. Please help us!

Today, I pray for those who imagine that they do not need You, who do not know what they are missing. I pray for those who are so close to You they could reach out and touch You if they only acknowledged Your holiness. I pray for those who believe they are alone in the world and that no one cares about them. I pray they would find You right now, today, and know that You have already supplied a net to rescue them. I pray they would seek truth and light and love and no longer live in a heartless world.

Amen.

Shaped and Molded

· ·

Oh yes, you shaped me first inside, then out;
you formed me in my mother's womb.
PSALM 139:13 MSG

Father in heaven,

I laugh at myself sometimes because I walk around as a human *doing*—doing whatever it is I imagine I should do and being so busy I forget the most important thing. . .that I'm a human *being*. As a human being, I need to seek my rest and my awareness of life and my options for living from You. I need to look to You to help me grow and move and live with integrity.

How can I forget that You formed me in my mother's womb? You protected me and nurtured me and made certain that I would come into the world whole and perfect. You did that; and ever since I was born, You've been trying to make sure that when I go out of the world, I will leave whole and perfect. Without You, I have no air to breathe, no ability to move, no knowledge of what to do next.

I pray for all Your children who know that Your hand is on their lives, that You have a purpose for them, and that You designed them with absolutely everything they need to get the job done. I pray that they will look at themselves from the inside out so that they can see how much You cherish them and how close You are to their hearts. I ask for Your mercy, grace, and blessing as You mold and shape each of us to be all that You want us to be.

Amen.

A Gentle Listener

Dear Lord,

Ah, there it is! You have guided us to keep cool, be patient, and listen more than we speak. You showed us by the example of Jesus that even when You are being falsely accused or when people simply don't know what they are talking about, the best defense is to stay calm and refuse to give in to any form of disruptive temper.

How I wish that more people listened to Your advice! We seem to have a temperamental planet where everybody walks around with a short fuse and nobody listens to anybody else. The talkers just get louder to hear the sound of their own voices, and the bullies just want to feel more powerful because they already know how weak they are.

Lord, let us be people who are gentle listeners, who try harder to hear each other and to hear Your wisdom in every circumstance. Help us to remain calm and patient in the face of adversity and never to give in to the taunts and ridicule of those who simply do not know any better. Help us to stand firm for what we believe, share our thoughts with patience, and make a difference because we have a heart shaped by Your hand.

Amen.

Fully Aware of You

*So know that the LORD your God is God, the faithful God.
He will keep his agreement of love for a thousand lifetimes
for people who love him and obey his commands.*

DEUTERONOMY 7:9 NCV

Father God,

I gave my heart to You a long time ago, and I realize that I don't always reflect that experience in my everyday life. I go about my business, thinking I have important things to do and that I won't be at peace unless I achieve my goals. I know it's important to live with a purpose, especially when we strive to live with Your purpose, but I also know how far I fall from the mark.

Oh, sure, I'm looking for You most of the time and asking for Your help and seeking Your guidance; but I'm pretty sure I'm still a long way from the bar that You have set for me. In fact, I am somewhat uncertain as to what I can achieve to please You, so I strive to draw nearer to You.

Your faithfulness is what keeps me going. I want to do the things that show You I love You and am willing to obey Your direction for my life. I want to shout out loud, "You are God!" and tell the world about incredible You.

Thank You for Your steadfast presence in my life and for Your willingness to forgive me when I'm wrong and love me into doing a better job. You are beyond my comprehension and wonderfully knowable at the same time. Help me to know You better today.

Amen.

Gluten Free

. . . .

*Do not let all kinds of strange teachings lead you into
the wrong way. Your hearts should be strengthened
by God's grace, not by obeying rules about foods,
which do not help those who obey them.*

HEBREWS 13:9 NCV

Dear Lord,

We spend a lot of time these days reading the labels of the foods we eat, counting the calories and the salt and the carbohydrates, and trying to make healthy choices. We study up on what is best for us to eat, yet many of us are still starving.

We are not starving because we lack the best ways to prepare potatoes but because we have not been nourished and strengthened by Your Spirit. We have thought so much about doing the right thing for our bodies in terms of what we eat that we neglected to do the right things for our souls.

Today I pray that You would help us to seek Your teachings, Your direction, Your ways to strengthen not only our hearts and minds but our eternal spirits as well. I pray for each person who wants to live a healthy and God-fearing life, and I ask that You would inspire each one to want to study more about You and live according to Your will and purpose. Thank You, dear Lord, for giving us a chance to be more than gluten free—we can be guilt free because of Jesus' sacrifice and love.

Amen.

Coming Up for Air

They would have been like a flood drowning us;
they would have poured over us like a river. They
would have swept us away like a mighty stream.

_{PSALM 124:4–5 NCV}

Dear Lord,

Some days I feel like I can hardly breathe. It takes everything I've got to walk around and do the most menial tasks. I don't know how to pray or what to say because I'm just overwhelmed with life and I'm not sure what to do next. As I float along on my man-made life raft, I start to think about Jesus. What would Jesus do now to get past all these sinking feelings? What would He suggest to help me feel safe and secure again?

These feelings are not just mine though. I read the papers and social media sites, and I can hear the same cries from others. So many people are drowning in fear and in heartbreak and in sins too numerous to mention. We are lost and need You, Lord, to be not only a life raft but a life preserver.

Help Your children today who are out of sorts, desperate to find their way again in more peaceful waters. We're in over our heads, Lord, and the only one who can save us from drowning is You. I pray You will reach down and pull us up to You and embrace us so that nothing can wash us away from Your hand. I ask for Your help so that all Your children can come up for air today and live in peace.

Amen.

When the Light Goes Out

. . . .

*"Those who fight against the light do not
know God's ways or stay in his paths."*
JOB 24:13 NCV

Dear God,

When the clouds move in and I cannot sense the moon or the stars or Your love anymore, it is overwhelming. It causes my heart to grieve, and even things that usually allow me to rejoice seem to be of little importance. It's not easy to walk the paths of life when we feel surrounded by the darkness.

Charles Spurgeon once wrote, "The night shall not hang in darkness forever over our souls; the sun shall yet arise with healing beneath its wings." With this thought, I sit quietly waiting for the sun, knowing that Your Son sees me and will prevail once more in time. I know that soon the clouds will disperse and I'll be able to feel the warmth of Your presence as it shines on my face.

I pray for everyone who sits in the gloom and the darkness, those who may be lonely or imprisoned by fear or hatred. I pray for those who can no longer see that a new day will come and that You will win the day. Help us to know Your ways and stay on Your paths. Help us to fight the darkness and return to Your precious light. I ask for Your favor on Your children around the world today.

Amen.

Stormy Weather

The disciples went and woke him, saying, "Master, Master, we're going to drown!" He got up and rebuked the wind and the raging waters; the storm subsided, and all was calm.

LUKE 8:24 NIV

Dear Lord of peace,

We long for certain peace to penetrate our hearts and give us a sense of safety and knowledge that all is well. We hope that we will somehow move swiftly over the waters of adversity and the storms that come to us in unexpected measure. Help us to stay calm wherever we may be today. Help us to rest in the assurance that Your presence in our lives will be sufficient to thwart any sudden storms.

You give us peace in times of trouble. When storms are around us, piercing the sky with flashes of light, rumbling across the clouds in harsh tones that vibrate the place where we stand, then we look to You to rebuke them. We look to You to calm the chaos and grant us the peace that only You can offer.

May everyone who seeks You to bring calm and order and comfort to life find You today. May everyone who wonders what they will do to escape those moments when nothing feels safe and when promises of better days slip through their fingers look for You. May they find You waiting lovingly and quietly deep within their hearts, ready to calm any storm and bring them peace again. I ask this, Father, in Jesus' name!

Amen.

What about Tomorrow?

· ·

"Therefore do not worry about tomorrow, for tomorrow will
worry about itself. Each day has enough trouble of its own."
MATTHEW 6:34 NIV

Dear Lord,

I would love to tell You that I am finally free of worry. I don't let the news of the day pierce my peace. I don't let the family crisis of the moment strip away my sense of love and security. I don't let the troubles all around me come and camp in my living room.

I'd like to be able to say all those things because I know that worrying is not right. Worrying means that I am not trusting You and that I have not spent enough time in prayer or in Your Word. Worrying means that I'm trying too hard to fix the world all by myself and that I've left You out of the equation.

It's no wonder You keep trying to get me to stop worrying. When I'm wrapped around worry, I'm not wrapped around You. I'm not allowing You to work in my heart and bring me a sense of joy that things will be better tomorrow.

As human beings, we have a lot of things to worry about. On the surface, it almost seems odd to try to prevent worry. After all, worrying means we care, right? The problem is that we take yesterday's worries and add them to the ones we have today that we'll also take into tomorrow, and we're left wondering why we can no longer function well. We lose heart. We lose our way. Help us to stay close to You when troubles come and to grasp Your hand until we are at peace again.

Amen.

More Life Lessons

*I know how to live when I am poor, and I know how to live
when I have plenty. I have learned the secret of being happy
at any time in everything that happens, when I have enough
to eat and when I go hungry, when I have more than I need
and when I do not have enough. I can do all things through
Christ, because he gives me strength.*

PHILIPPIANS 4:12–13 NCV

Father in heaven,

One of the best lessons in this life is the one we need to grasp with our whole heart, the one that reminds us to be content in all situations. I can be content, not because I have answers to every conflict or because help will come swiftly when troubles abound; no, I can be content because You are there, and in You I find the strength to carry on. In You I have hope, and so I can set an expectation that things will change and that happiness will come again.

From any window around the world, we can look out and see trouble. We can see the people who live in great need and the ones who live in the mansions on the hills. What we know, though, is that the only people experiencing true happiness are those who live with You, inviting You into all their life circumstances. Whether they dine with kings or those gathered in a homeless shelter, they can smile.

I pray for those who need new reasons to smile today. I pray their hearts will be lighter as You lift them above whatever circumstance they may have and give them a greater measure of Your strength. Thank You, Lord.

Amen.

A Healthy Heart

Jesus heard this and said to them, "It is not the healthy
people who need a doctor, but the sick. I did not come
to invite good people but to invite sinners."

MARK 2:17 NCV

Heavenly Father,

When You breathed life into us, You did so with such love and
compassion that we couldn't help but feel the gift of Your presence.
You are the air we breathe and our opportunity to be lifted above
our average lives and do great things.

Our desire, then, is to offer a healthy demonstration to those
around us of who we are because of You. We want others to know
our stories so they can repeat them to their own friendship circle
and get the news out that You are alive and well. We want everyone to know that "the doctor is in" and no one needs to suffer
needlessly ever again.

Thank You for calling us to Your side, checking on us, and
giving us an eternal bill of health as we live in the world. Help us
to breathe in Your Spirit, soak in Your Word, and fill the air around
us with hope because of You and all You've done to heal our hearts
and our hurts.

I pray for everyone today who needs to have a stronger heart,
better health, and more opportunity to know You. I ask that You
heal each of us so that we can be Your remedy for an ailing world.

Amen.

Smoke and Mirrors

. . . .

Blessed is the man to whom the LORD does not impute
iniquity, and in whose spirit there is no deceit.
PSALM 32:2 NKJV

Dear Lord,

I don't know how many times I've been duped by a smooth-talking sales pitch. I was probably an easy mark because I wasn't prepared for the pressure they would put on me to buy their bill of goods. I may have been so excited to buy a new car or make a great deal that I didn't pay attention to the details or read the fine print until my name was already on the dotted line. There are a lot of deals made in this world by those who are really good at manipulating smoke and mirrors.

I pray for the Spirit of truth to surround each person I love today. Help them to be able to discern the difference of whether any negotiation they make is a good deal or not. Give them spiritual eyes to see exactly what they need to know before they commit to something that's difficult to leave behind.

I pray for all those who put their trust in You so they would not be misled by the words of another person. I pray they would see more clearly the path You have set and not be manipulated from that path. I pray we will understand that the only place where the grass is greener is in Your care and keeping. You know what we need, and You know the best way for us to get the deal of a lifetime. It all begins with You. Thank You, Father, for offering us truth!

Amen.

An Open Letter

Whatever things are true, whatever things are noble, whatever things are just, whatever things are pure, whatever things are lovely, whatever things are of good report, if there is any virtue and if there is anything praiseworthy—meditate on these things.

PHILIPPIANS 4:8 NKJV

Lord God,

You wrote a love letter on our hearts the day You redeemed us through Jesus. Your love letter remains the same now as it was when You first penned it and brought it into being. It says that no matter what we go through, You'll be there. It reminds us that whatever happens we can depend on You. It is an open letter of trust and love and compassion, and we know that nothing can keep us from You.

Help us to read Your letter a bit every day. Help us to digest the words in a way that nourishes our spirits and gives us the best chance to have a balanced life. I pray that You would be the voice we hear, the words we read, the beauty we see, the opportunity ahead, and the passion of our souls no matter where we are and what we do.

Give us peace today so we can meditate on those things that are good for our hearts and strengthen our commitment to You. Bless the things that are noble and true and lovely so that we can receive them in utter joy each day. Thank You for addressing Your special love letter even to me.

Amen.

Do You See Me?

But whoever has this world's goods, and sees his
brother in need, and shuts up his heart from him,
how does the love of God abide in him?

1 JOHN 3:17 NKJV

Dear Lord,

In our longing to live lives that are shaped more by our hearts than our intellect, more by compassion than by selfishness, and more by Your Spirit than ours, we look to You to help us transform any stubbornness we may be holding on to and to change us into something more beautiful. We look to You to create a clean heart within us so that when we look at ourselves in the mirror, we can see the person You see, the person who cares about the needs of those we meet each day.

There are times when we feel overwhelmed by the needs of others, knowing that we can't help everyone, but encourage us to be willing to give what we can to those who have greater needs than we do ourselves. Help us to be examples of Your light and Your steadfast love.

We know that whatever we have of this world's goods won't last. What lasts are those things we do out of kindness and love. Those are the things that become warm memories, our legacy, and the things that give us a sense of joy and fuel our desire to do all the good we can wherever we are.

Help each of us to see ourselves as givers and encouragers and as people who love others with our whole heart.

Amen.

Heart Attack

· ·

God, you are my comfort when
I am very sad and when I am afraid.

JEREMIAH 8:18 NCV

Dear God,

I have trouble watching the news. It seems like there's always more sadness and loss and anger and violence being reported than anything else. Where is the good news? Where are the people who are excited about life and who are doing all they can to make the world a better place with their favorite charity or in support of a good cause?

I like to think that human beings are capable of amazing compassion and kindness. You have given us multiple examples of what it means to be giving and loving to each other. You have instructed us in how to live so that we can live well upon the earth.

Help us to hear Your voice today. Help us to lift the sadness that permeates so many hearts around the globe and offer them Your comfort and Your peace. Let us so desire to honor You in the things we do that we can't help but embrace each other in the process and thereby subdue the fears that abound.

I pray for everyone who feels sad or afraid, Lord, and ask that You would let them feel Your warmth and Your love and comfort. I praise You and thank You for drawing near when we need You.

Amen.

Wounded and Healed

. . . .

"Blessed is the one whom God corrects; so do not despise the discipline of the Almighty. For he wounds, but he also binds up; he injures, but his hands also heal."

JOB 5:17–18 NIV

Lord God,

There's no doubt that a good father who loves his children must help to guide them through discipline. Discipline is not something any of us truly embrace. We don't always understand it, sometimes we're not sure why we deserve it, and other times we simply wish we didn't have to endure it.

The fact is we usually benefit from discipline that is fair and administered in a loving way. We can see the error of our ways more clearly and recognize the things that got us into trouble so that we won't do those things again. The problem is that human beings don't always administer discipline with love. Perhaps we don't know how to do it in a way that is effective and strengthens the lesson to be learned.

When You discipline us to get us back on track, I pray that You might do so with compassion. Please recognize that we are sad when we do things that displease You and that we want to do better. Help us to heal from the wounds of life so that we embrace Your guidance and direction in positive ways. Help us to be Your healers with hands that bless others.

Amen.

Dancing with Life

You turned my wailing into dancing;
you removed my sackcloth and clothed me with joy.
PSALM 30:11 NIV

Lord of the dance,

One of the key things I've learned over the years is how important it is for any of us to strive for balance in our lives. We need to balance our work and play, our joy and sadness, and our moving fast and sitting still. We can be our best selves when we give our minds and bodies and spirits the greatest opportunity to function equally and well.

Oftentimes we are conflicted about how to achieve that balance. We manage it in one arena of our lives but not in another. If we get out and exercise, we still don't give up cigarettes. If we take time off to relax, we still spend hours thinking about work. If we are in a relationship, we take it for granted; and if we are not in a relationship that's meaningful to us, we pray for it to happen.

We are complex people who get some of it right and a lot of it wrong, and then we wonder when illness strikes or sadness sets in because we're suffering from the losses of time misspent. I pray today for all of us who seek a better balance in our lives and who want to be able to dance a bit more often. Remind us how we can best achieve a life clothed in joy.

Amen.

Bless the Children

. . . .

*But Jesus said, "Let the little children come to Me, and
do not forbid them; for of such is the kingdom of heaven."*
MATTHEW 19:14 NKJV

Dear Lord,

It encourages my heart to realize that You can call any of Your
children to come to You no matter what age they are. I am awed
when I see a young child who is simply in love with Jesus, trusting
and believing in Him with wholehearted joy. I long to have that
sense of You in my life today.

I pray today for those of us who are eager to draw near to
You. Help us to come with enthusiastic abandon as though we are
awaiting the arms of our best friend in the world. Give us a chance
to express our love and tell You the stories of all that has gone on
in our lives. Let us simply enjoy being close to You.

After we've had a chance to spend time with You, then send
us back into the world and help us to be more effective in sharing
our faith and our hearts with others. Help us to be eager to tell
the stories of all You've done in our lives to sustain us and guide
us toward our cherished dreams.

We all need You, Lord, and we need You with the same at-
tachment that any child has for a parent. We need to be near You,
feel Your presence, and know that we are never alone because
You are always there for us. Thank You for being such an amazing
and faithful Father.

Amen.

Why I'm Not Afraid

"Be strong and of good courage, do not fear nor be
afraid of them; for the LORD your God, He is the One
who goes with you. He will not leave you nor forsake you."

DEUTERONOMY 31:6 NKJV

Dear Faithful One,

Sometimes just stepping outside the door feels like I'm entering
a battle zone. My mind is filled with the news of the day—people in
poverty, wars around the world, and political agendas raging—and
I haven't even gotten out of the driveway. The traffic is congested
on the way to work, and no one seems to be in a friendly mood.
Could it be that we've all left home without protection? Could it
be that we've forgotten to ask Your help with the day and to seek
Your peace and patience?

Whatever I do today, Lord, please come with me. Please help me
fight any battles that I must face, whether they're minor conflicts at
work or stressful matters with my children or my spouse. Help me
and all the other people out there to recognize Your hand at work
in our lives. Let us put on the full armor of God so that anyplace
we happen to be today, we'll know we have Your protection and
that there is nothing we need to fear. It's a scary world, and the
last thing we want to do is leave home without Your strength and
guidance. Be with all of us today.

Amen.

Having a Circumcised Heart

And the LORD your God will circumcise your heart and the heart of your descendants, to love the LORD your God with all your heart and with all your soul, that you may live.

DEUTERONOMY 30:6 NKJV

Dear God,

I know that You first asked our ancestors to utilize circumcision to demonstrate their commitment to You. You wanted them to be a people set apart who knew that You were God and they were Your people.

After You sent Jesus into the world, You let us show our devotion to You through our love for Him and through our faith in You. You asked us to worship You with our hearts and minds and souls.

As I think about the idea of having a heart that is circumcised, it reminds me that because of Jesus I, too, belong to You as a person set apart to share the good news and to tell the stories of all You've done in my life. You have created a clean heart within me so that I can honor You with my life, my actions, and my words.

Thank You for Jesus. Thank You for giving all of us a way to be one of Your children. Thank You for shaping our hearts and minds so that we can live with You forever. My soul rejoices as I praise You and thank You for the gift of eternal love that began right here on earth when I asked You to come into my heart. Bless everyone who seeks You with their whole heart today.

Amen.

Guide My Steps

Look at me and have mercy on me as you do for those who love you. Guide my steps as you promised; don't let any sin control me.
PSALM 119:132–133 NCV

Dear God,

I confess I'm not very good at reading directions. If I have an idea about how to put something together, even if there's an instruction guide, I'll usually just try to assemble all the pieces myself. When it doesn't work out, I go back and read the directions. The sad part is that I didn't have to do it wrong to begin with because the directions were right in front of me. They even said "Read first before you attempt to assemble this product."

I admit that there are times when I do the same thing to You. You're near me, right in front of me and beside me, and yet I will try to assemble the pieces of my life all by myself. I imagine that I have a good idea about how things should go, and so I think it will save me time to just get to it and do it. The problem is, when I don't get all the pieces put together in the right way, then I have to go back and try again. That's when I find myself praying and asking for Your guidance, waiting for Your instruction.

Help me to seek You first in all the things I'm trying to do. Help me not assume I know where I'm going. I pray for Your guidance in all the areas of my life, and I pray that Your presence will be felt in the hearts and minds of believers everywhere. Help all of us to seek Your advice and Your will for every step we take so we can complete our tasks in ways that please You. Thank You for loving us so much and for always being ready to guide us as we go forward.

Amen.

Put Me In, Coach!

Then I heard the Lord's voice, saying, "Whom can I send?
Who will go for us?" So I said, "Here I am. Send me!"
ISAIAH 6:8 NCV

Heavenly Father,

You know me better than I know myself. You know when it's time for me to suit up and get into the game and when it's better for me to sit on the sidelines. You bring opportunities my way and give me a chance to determine my interest in pursuing them. When it comes to my life activities and resources and relationships, I think our system works well.

However, when it comes to serving You with my whole heart and mind and soul, I imagine that I may sit on the sidelines a bit too much. I'm in the ballpark, but I'm not always ready to play; and when things get a little crazy all around me, I tend to retreat more than get into the game.

Today, Lord, I ask You to give me a willing heart, one that is suited up all the time, ready to play whenever the whistle blows. I know there's more that I can do, and when I'm in the game, I see those opportunities all around me. When I spend too much time on the bench, I miss the calls going on and sometimes I don't even see the plays. Put me in, Coach! Help me to be a great team player, because I can see the need all around me. Whether I'm on the field or on the bench, let my heart be prepared anytime to accept Your call to help those around me. Help all believers so that we'll try harder today to get into the game and win more hearts for You.

Amen.

This Little Light of Mine!

The LORD is my light and the one who saves me.
So why should I fear anyone? The LORD protects
my life. So why should I be afraid?

PSALM 27:1 NCV

Dear God,

I remember when I was a child and I first sang a song called "This Little Light of Mine." I sang it with gusto because I wanted to shine my light for You for the rest of my life. When I think about that song now, it still makes me smile, but it also serves as a reminder.

That particular song helps me remember You in a childlike faith kind of way, a way that says I trust You to protect me and that I have nothing to fear as long as I lean into Your light. It's a reminder that I want to pass the light along to those around me so that they can be warmed by its glow and stand ready to shine for You.

Help me to allow my light to shine more brightly on the people I meet today. Help me to have that same innocent faith that simply wants to take Your beautiful message and share it the best way that I can. Let me shine for You so that Your name continues to be praised all around the world. I pray that nothing will ever put out this little light of mine! I praise You and adore You. Thank You for saving me all those years ago. You are my light!

Amen.

Working for You

*Whatever you do, work at it with all
your heart, as working for the Lord.*
COLOSSIANS 3:23 NIV

Dear Lord,

When I take the time to really think about the work I do and the things that motivate me to do that work, I realize that my perspective may be off a bit. I may be missing the most important ingredient. It isn't about my time and how I spend it. It isn't about my need for financial stability. It isn't even that I have a particular talent to do the job I do. When I look at my work in terms of time or money or talent, I miss the most needful thing. I miss putting You at the top of my equation. I miss the realization that I don't work for the tax man and I don't work to try to climb some elusive ladder. I work for You.

What does it mean for me to have work that I do for You? It means that I start with You each day. I bring You into every part of my workspace and make sure that I'm doing what You would have me do. It means I seek You out for guidance and strength and stamina when a project takes too long or I have lost patience with my work environment. It means that every word I speak, and every insight I share with others, has only one objective. I want to please my Boss. I want to please You.

Lord, help me to work with my whole heart for only one reason—so that I can serve You better and I can help others know Your name.

Amen.

Heart Failure

For troubles without number surround me; my sins have overtaken me, and I cannot see. They are more than the hairs of my head, and my heart fails within me.

PSALM 40:12 NIV

Dear God,

Sometimes, whether we like it or not, life goes haywire, and we realize we contributed our share to making the craziness happen. Of course, we like to think that we're staying on the path You designed and paying attention to the words that come out of our mouths or the actions we take. We like to think we're aware all the time of letting Your light shine and tucking our sins in so they don't show. The problem is that we have to own those sins. Help us bring them before You and drop them at Your feet and seek Your mercy.

Help us be people You can be proud of, the ones who pray through temptation and strive to bring peace to troubling situations. Help us draw close to You all the time so that we know instantly when we've fallen short of the mark.

Lord, I'm not sure I have it in me to live a life or even a day without some thought, some action, some word, or some grievous sin overtaking me; but Lord, when that happens, I pray You will help to cleanse my heart and mind with Your love and mercy and cause me to walk in ways that please You and bring glory to Your name. I seek Your grace and favor for all those I love as well.

Amen.

A Heart-Shaped Faith

*The word that saves is right here, as near as the tongue
in your mouth, as close as the heart in your chest.
It's the word of faith that welcomes God.*

ROMANS 10:8 MSG

Lord God,

Faith is a mysterious and wonderful thing! You designed our hearts so we could receive You in faith. You gave us the gift of being able to perceive and acknowledge and lift up our spirits to You as though we are one. You have given each of us a chance to have a heart-shaped faith.

Today, Lord, I pray that You would strengthen my faith so that I see Your face in every person I pass by on the street. I pray that I would hear Your voice as I hold conversations with people who are dear to me. I pray that I would touch Your heart with each opportunity I have to give something of myself to the people around me; and I pray for a measure of grace for those times when I neglect the very faith that sustains me.

Be near to all the believers who seek to walk with You. Help them to live in such a way that no one would ever be able to doubt that they belong to You. Fill each heart with a certain joy and a bountiful measure of Your Holy Spirit so that we pass along this gift of faith to those who are eager to receive it. Help all of us to honor Your name as we go about our day and to hold fast to Your steadfast love with every beat of our hearts.

Amen.

On Cruise Control

*Keep your eyes focused on what is right,
and look straight ahead to what is good.*

PROVERBS 4:25 NCV

Dear Lord,

Sometimes I feel like I'm living on cruise control. I just set the speed limit of my day and start moving. It works for a while, but then I realize I've let a number of hours simply evaporate without any real notice of where they went or whether I used them wisely. I kept going, but I'm not sure what I accomplished.

Today I pray that You would help me and all of us who seek Your guidance to stop moving on cruise control and instead to be intentional about knowing You are in control. When we know that You are in control, the day takes on a different meaning. We look at others with a heart to see them as You see them. We look at ourselves with a bit more forgiveness and try harder to do as much good as we can do. We aren't just cruising along; we're walking along with You.

It's great to be focused on the things that must be accomplished, looking straight ahead to try to get to our goals, but help us to want even more than that. Help us to know that we spend our time well when we are doing the work You called us to do and causing others to become more aware of Your goodness and Your divine love in the process. Give us hearts to let You be totally in control today. Thank You for keeping us on the right path each day.

Amen.

I Did It Again

We all make many mistakes. If people never said anything wrong, they would be perfect and able to control their entire selves, too.

JAMES 3:2 NCV

Father God,

I'm never happy when I do things that are just plain stupid, things that I know I should never have allowed to happen. I wonder at myself that I can get tripped up so easily. I wonder how You keep forgiving me over and over again.

The humbling part of realizing these things is that my heart is reminded that I need to be as gentle with others who make mistakes as I hope You will be with me when I make a mess of things. I need to step aside from the action that made me unhappy and look with love at the person who needs my forgiveness. You do it all the time, and believe me, I'm truly grateful for that.

I pray for all of us to be more forgiving of each other. Whether we do big things or small things that cause sadness or anger or dismay, I ask You to remind us that we are all people and people make mistakes. Thank You for being the one who forgives us anytime our hearts are willing to surrender the unfortunate mistakes we've made. Thank You for helping us to rise again so that we can try to do better the next time. Help us to be kinder and more forgiving to those around us. Heal our relationships quickly anytime our hearts are grieved by foolishness. Help us to be more like You.

Amen.

Spread the Love

"The Lord has filled my heart with joy;
I feel very strong in the Lord."

1 Samuel 2:1 NCV

Father in heaven,

It's not every day that I wake up feeling strong and ready to take on the world. On days like this, I sense Your anointing and realize that with You in my life, all things are possible. I can cast aside my doubts and worries and simply spread the love You have given all of us even when we're not paying attention.

I pray for strength for each person who steps out in faith to do the work of their hands. I pray that they would discover more of what it means to have You walk beside them as they go about their daily routines. I pray that their hearts would be filled to over-flowing as they stand firm on Your truth and seek to be kinder to those around them.

Thank You for always being there, guiding and inspiring our hearts to do better and to give every measure of grace and love more intentionally. Thank You for shining a light that helps us to walk through the shadows knowing full well that You are there to protect us. I pray that Your strength and Your protection and Your love will shine on all those who seek to do Your will and who simply need You by their side.

Bless all people in Your care, and fill their hearts with joy.

Amen.

Seeing from the Inside Out

"God does not see the same way people see. People look at the outside of a person, but the LORD looks at the heart."

1 SAMUEL 16:7 NCV

Dear Lord,

I'm grateful that You know a person's heart. What that means to me is that You know what motivates actions and what causes grief. You know what creates distance and what communicates love. You know that everything we do is some function of where we exist at a heart level.

Today, my prayers are for all of us to want hearts that are motivated to please You and to love You. Help us to then turn around and do all we can to extend the hands and heart of fellowship to those around us. Help us to desire to give more than we receive and to plant more than we sow. Encourage us to be people with hearts that are compassionate and kind.

The world is harsh, and we experience its drama every day. We cannot see into the hearts of those who stir up strife and hatred. We cannot see what causes them to be cruel to others and what drives them to seek power. Only You can see us from the inside out. Help us to seek Your power, the kind that drives us to do good and to want love to direct our steps. Help us to see each person we encounter today with Your eyes. Protect us and forgive us; bind our hearts together in love for Your name's sake.

Amen.

Where Are You When I Cry?

*"There must be Someone in heaven who
knows the truth about me, in highest heaven,
some Attorney who can clear my name—my Champion,
my Friend, while I'm weeping my eyes out before GOD."*

JOB 16:19–20 MSG

Dear Lord,

I pray today for Your children around the world who seek Your face. They bow before You with hearts that are wounded and broken. They live with uncertainty and fear, and they wonder if You can hear them as they cry. Sadly, these children are many, and in their humanness, they cry for the same reasons. They seek peace in their lives and joy in their spirits. They seek You for daily bread and for basic needs to survive.

Help us to trust in You completely for the sake of Your Son, Jesus, and for the sake of each person who needs to embrace You. Help us to see Your face in every person who aspires to know more of You and who cries over the pain and suffering of life. You are the hope we can feel through our tears when illness strikes or losses overwhelm us. You are the one who can inspire us to keep trying and trusting and believing.

When we come before You, Lord, please draw near and let us feel Your embrace. Let us know that You share our tears and that You are acting even as we cry to help a smile return to our faces. We need You, and we know that You are our champion and friend. Thank You for watching over us.

Amen.

Humble Hearts

*"I give new life to those who are humble
and to those whose hearts are broken."*

Isaiah 57:15 NCV

Dear God,

There's nothing like a broken heart to give us a humble spirit. It's often in our brokenness that we understand more clearly what little power we actually have in this world. We know that You are in control; and even when we don't like our circumstances, we know that there is only one thing to do. We must bring our messy, broken, out-of-control lives and lay them at Your feet. We must seek Your compassion and mercy and grace with humble hearts.

Thank You for being with all of us who suffer from injustice or unkindness or fear of some kind. Thank You for holding us up to the light and giving us the strength we need to keep trying.

We pray that You would grant us new life. Grant us the kind of life that recognizes Your Spirit in the faces of others. Give us wisdom and compassion so that when we speak and when we act, we do so in ways that please You. Give us humble hearts so that we can try to think and act and walk in the ways of Jesus.

As the days pass swiftly by, it can feel like we are simply spinning along, disconnected and alone. Help us to know that we are never alone, for You have already redeemed us so that we can live in peace and in Your glory. Thank You for the new life we only can have in You.

Amen.

I Got It All Wrong

Forgive me this wrong!
2 CORINTHIANS 12:13 NKJV

Father in heaven,

It's never easy to have to admit when I do things that I know are just wrong. They may not be big things, at least the kind of things other people would notice, but they are still wrong. You have continued to pour out Your mercy on me, not despite the things I do that grieve Your Spirit, but because of Your love and Your compassion. You keep holding me up and pointing me in the right direction, and I praise and thank You for that.

I ask Your forgiveness today for those little things that I do that my heart recognizes right away as wrong. Whether I said something that was mildly unkind, or whether I was not motivated by love in my thoughts or actions, I know I need Your forgiveness. When I do something that is driven by self-care or that is self-serving, I need Your help to remember who I am in You. In You, I am whole. Without You, I struggle to get along in the world because I allow one piece of my life to drive my actions. Help all of us who struggle with those pieces. When we worry too much or suffer illness or loss or financial stress, those pieces start to rule our actions. Those pieces keep us from receiving Your help. Those pieces often prompt us to do the wrong things.

Forgive us when we take our eyes off You and focus too much on the things of this world. Help each of us when we simply get it all wrong!

Amen.

Peeling Off the Labels

"Forgive and treat each person as he should be treated because you know what is in a person's heart. Only you know what is in everyone's heart."

1 KINGS 8:39 NCV

Dear God,

We live in a culture that loves to identify and classify and label nearly everything. We pride ourselves on assessing people and things quickly and having a sense of the good and the bad and the ugly. We like knowing we can embrace or dismiss each other simply because we've assigned a label that makes our actions appropriate.

There is a problem with this, though. Sometimes we're wrong. We can assume the wrong things about a person based on the way they wear their hair or the style of their clothes. We can imagine that we know how they think and how they feel because we recognize their position in the workplace or their level of authority. We often treat others on our assumptions of who we believe they are. The truth is we don't know what is inside a person's heart. We don't always know what motivates their actions or what causes them to be in dire circumstances. We don't have insider information on every soul we might meet on any given day. We don't know them, but You do.

Lord, today I pray that we would each seek to know the heart of people we connect with on a regular basis and that we would try harder to understand others before we attach labels to them. Help us to look for the good in each other and then to treat each other with love.

Amen.

In Awe and Wonder

. . . .

"You must honor the LORD and truly serve him with all your heart.
Remember the wonderful things he did for you!"

1 SAMUEL 12:24 NCV

Dear heavenly Father,

My heart is bursting with love today. I'm overwhelmed by a sense of Your goodness and Your kindness to me. I understand like I may never have realized before that there is nothing in my life that is not part of Your plan. You created everything, and in the process, You gave me the freedom to choose You. You allowed me the growing room to try to figure things out and to learn about You little by little. The more I learned, the more You showed me. The more You showed me, the more I stood in awe of Your mighty works.

Some may not give You the credit for the things You do for us, all of us, every single day. You provide for our basic needs, keeping us warm and well fed and protected. You see us right where we are, knowing exactly what we need, and often guide us along a secure path before we even realize what You have done.

Help us to remember the things You do. Remind us how You stepped in when we weren't sure which way to go, or when You provided for our well-being through an unexpected source. Teach us to open our eyes to see You when we're feeling somewhat alone or uncertain. You are the source of all we are and all we can be. Let all of us share the stories of Your love every chance we get. Let our hearts serve You and celebrate You with unending joy. I praise You and thank You with all my heart.

Amen.

Only on Your Wings

*"As an eagle stirs up its nest, hovers over its young,
spreading out its wings, taking them up, carrying
them on its wings, so the LORD alone led him."*

DEUTERONOMY 32:11–12 NKJV

Dear Lord,

When I imagine Your Spirit drawing close to me, hovering over me like a protective mother, spreading Your wings to keep me safe and carrying me from place to place, I have that peace that passes all understanding. I have a sense of comfort, and I long to embrace You even more, to relax in Your care and let You lead me to the places You alone know are best for me.

I so often forget that I am not the eagle but only the little bird. I am not the one who can control the situations around me or the one who knows the best direction for my circumstances. I cannot even feather my own nest without You.

I pray that You will lead me and that You will go ahead of Your children everywhere who seek Your direction and need so desperately to fly to safety in the comfort of Your wings. I pray that You will help us to trust You no matter what stirs our nests, no matter what troubles may loom and cause us fear. Be our strength and our portion, and take us up with You to live more wholly and more completely through Your will and mercy. I ask You this for the sake of each person whose heart needs to rest beneath Your wings today.

Amen.

Worthy of Acceptance

This is a faithful saying and worthy of all acceptance.
For to this end we both labor and suffer reproach,
because we trust in the living God, who is the
Savior of all men, especially of those who believe.

1 TIMOTHY 4:9–10 NKJV

Dear God,

Some days I can boldly and truthfully say out loud, "I trust in the living God." It feels good to be able to say so and to mean it. It feels important to my heart and mind and soul to know that You are the Savior of all of us and that You have drawn believers to You from all over the globe.

The odd thing is that there are days also when I let life overwhelm me and I let uncertainty spin its webs of fear and doubt. At those times, I am at the mercy of every wind that blows, and evil can triumph simply because I've lost my bearings. Forgive me for those days and those moments when I take You for granted or when I don't show You that I trust You for every part of my life. I know that on those days, it is You and You alone who hold fast to me and sustain me.

You are the one who called me by name a long time ago—the one who has been shaping my heart and mind ever since. You are the one who lifts my spirit over the bumps and bruises life brings and gives me reason to hope once again. You are the living God, and today I seek Your favor and Your mercy for every person who believes in You with all their heart and mind and soul. Bless each one, and help them to accept the truth of all You are.

Amen.

Lift Me Up to Where You Are

God protects me like a shield;
he saves those whose hearts are right.

PSALM 7:10 NCV

Father in heaven,

My prayer today is to have a "heart that is right." As I look to You to help me live a heart-shaped life, I realize that I need Your constant and continual guidance. I need You to be my source of inspiration so I desire to live in ways that please You. I need You to keep me on track and to offer me forgiveness when I move off the path.

Sometimes I try to imagine what it means to have a heart that is right. I look at people who are kind and giving, who offer a helping hand to others, and who embrace the positive things in life, and I assume their hearts are right. I may also look at people in authority who are benevolent to people and who do all they can to make life better for those in their care. I believe they are doing Your work and that their hearts are right.

Though I may not always know what defines a "right heart" in Your eyes, I believe that the one way I might define it is through Jesus. I pray for all of us who seek to have our hearts follow in His path and who want to be more like Him in the things we do. I pray that our hearts will be held in His love and protected for all our lives. Save us, and grant us the kind of heart that can only live through Your Son. Help us to then share our hearts and our love with those around us so they, too, might draw closer to Your salvation.

Amen.

Gifts of Light and Shadows

Every good gift and every perfect gift is from above,
and comes down from the Father of lights,
with whom there is no variation or shadow of turning.

JAMES 1:17 NKJV

Dear Father of lights,

I don't always think about what it means that You are the same God who created the universe and all that exists, the same God who has watched over humankind from the days of Adam, and that You do not change. You set the stars in the heavens and put the earth under Your feet, and You gave each one of us a place to live and grow and get to know You better.

You designed us, and You know our hearts. You gave us the gift of life and the opportunity to spend that gift wisely and well. We can choose at any time to live in abundance and fullness by Your grace and mercy, or we can choose to walk our own path. Either way, You are the one who does not change. Your love is steadfast, and Your gifts are everlasting.

Help me and the people I love to desire Your gifts, the ones that You meant for each of us to have. Give us wisdom to know how to use those gifts for the good of others, and most of all, guide us back to Yourself with grace and mercy. We may choose at times to walk in the shadows, but we are grateful to know that we can always find You when our hearts are determined to do so, for we can always draw nearer to Your light.

Thank You for Your incredible gifts to us.

Amen.

Ruling the Rulers

"I ask that you give me a heart that understands,
so I can rule the people in the right way and will know
the difference between right and wrong. Otherwise,
it is impossible to rule this great people of yours."

1 KINGS 3:9 NCV

Dear Lord,

We don't always know what guides the rulers of this world. Some seem driven by power, wanting to gain more and more of this world's lands and people simply to glorify themselves. Some lead with intellect, imagining that they know more than anyone else what is best for those they govern. A few rule in the same way that King Solomon ruled when he asked You to give him wisdom so that he could rule fairly and well.

I pray that You would rule over me and over all human beings. I pray that You would show Your power over those who rule with cruelty and greed as their chiefs of state. I pray that You would make all rulers powerless who work to deceive or harm the people around them. Help those who have enough intellect to know what is right to be able to accept Your guidance about how to achieve their goals.

Most of all, Lord, I pray for those leaders around the world who strive to rule others with wisdom. I pray that You would increase their abilities to govern and help them to know the difference between right and wrong. Give any person in power a wise and discerning heart. Help them to rule with Your authority and mercy.

Amen.

Be Wholly Holy!

Now may the God of peace make you holy in every way,
and may your whole spirit and soul and body be kept
blameless until our Lord Jesus Christ comes again.

1 THESSALONIANS 5:23 NLT

Gracious God of peace,

Whenever I'm confronted with the word *holy*, I'm immediately concerned that I've fallen way short of the mark. I can't even imagine that You see me as making much progress in my efforts to draw nearer to You so that I can understand what it truly means to be holy.

Forgive me for taking so long to recognize all that it takes to become a person who is wholly holy every day. In this greeting to the people of Thessalonica, the apostle Paul suggests that they strive to be kept blameless in every way. If being holy requires that we be blameless in body, mind, spirit, and soul, then few of us will ever achieve the goal. Even if we get it for a moment, we lose sight of it again. Staying holy until the day that Jesus returns feels truly impossible.

So help me to understand the ways that I can choose more intentionally to be holy. Help me to be aware of the things I do that may affect my mind and body and spirit in ways that are simply wrong for me. I pray for each person who desires to have a heart for holiness that You would guide and guard and tend to their needs today.

Amen.

Keeping Your Word

"My God, I want to do what you want.
Your teachings are in my heart."

PSALM 40:8 NCV

Dear God,

I suspect by now I should have a better understanding of what it is I think You want from me. I should be wise in the ways of my body, mind, and spirit because I've been walking with You for several years. The fact is that I believe with all my heart that I am meant to serve You and that I have a purpose ordained by You before I was even born. I am certain, then, that there are things You want from me.

My desire is to keep You first in my life and to please You. I want to be one of the people You can count on, no matter what the job is that needs to be done. I want to be willing to go the extra mile and to give spontaneously and lovingly in all circumstances. I want to make You proud of the things I do.

Sometimes, though, I confess that I don't fully realize what it is You do want. I get a glimpse of the ideas You have placed in my mind and heart, and I start to run with them, hoping to please You with my efforts, only to fall short once again. Help me to be a good listener when You call my name. Help me to stand firmly on Your Word and on Your teachings. Help me to live and to love as only You would have me do. I *seek* Your humble favor on my life and on the work of my hands.

Amen.

Manage My Expectations

"I say this because I know what I am planning for you,"
says the LORD. "I have good plans for you, not plans
to hurt you. I will give you hope and a good future."
JEREMIAH 29:11 NCV

Dear Lord,

It's a new day, and I want to move through it with a positive spirit and a heart to serve You. I have a laundry list of things to do and work to be done, and it all feels good. I thank You for giving me the kinds of tasks that make me happy and give me a sense of fulfillment. I thank You for knowing me so well that You guide me carefully along each day.

Today I pray that You will bless all those who seek You and help them to manage their expectations, knowing that whatever they do with a positive spirit and in keeping with Your guidance will prosper them. I pray that You will grant each one fulfilling moments and opportunities to do good.

So often the news of the day weakens our spirits and causes us to either assume the worst or to simply have no expectation of good things that could come our way. We start to imagine that the best news is that nothing terrible or evil came our way. I ask that You cover us over with Your mercy and grace so that we would not allow those negative thoughts to permeate our lives and destroy our desire to serve You. I pray that You would watch over our hopes and our desires to make a difference wherever we are. I thank You for giving each of us new hope and possibility. I praise Your name!

Amen.

To Pray or Not to Pray

Pray in the Spirit at all times with all kinds of prayers,
asking for everything you need. To do this you must always
be ready and never give up. Always pray for all God's people.

EPHESIANS 6:18 NCV

Dear God,

Help me today to foster an attitude of prayer. If I'm going to be ready at any moment to pray for myself or for the needs of others, then I ask You to soften my heart and cause me to see the needs for prayer wherever I may be. I realize that my prayer life is something that has to be trained and genuinely desired. I want to be Your prayer servant, available to pray anytime for those I love and for those You love.

I offer You my heart and ask You to reshape any aspect of it that resists an opportunity to pray. Flood my mind with the needs of others so that I can come to You whether on my knees or at work or driving in my car to seek Your help and Your presence.

I know that everything is in Your hands and that there is truly nothing You desire from me if my heart and spirit are not part of it. Show me the ways I can pray and the people I can pray for today. Grant me the grace and the love and the deepest desire to be an intercessor and a prayer warrior wherever You might lead me. If any doubt assails me, Lord, then I ask You to accept my prayers of faith and to wash away any doubts that would keep me from this task. Thank You for being so willing to hear the prayers of Your children.

Amen.

Wet Clay

. . . .

Shall what is formed say to the one who formed it, "You did not make me"? Can the pot say to the potter, "You know nothing"?
ISAIAH 29:16 NIV

Creator God,

Thank You for making us flexible and changeable, like wet cement or clay. Show us the ways that You would like us to stretch and bend or grow and move. Grant us the willingness to allow You to mold our hearts and minds so that we become more beautiful in Your sight.

I ask that You, as our heavenly designer, help each of us to be vessels of joy and grace, causing our hearts to be merciful to each other, keeping us in Your hands so that we can be reshaped without being broken. Take away our brittle thoughts and stubborn ideas. Grant that we would see others as being renewed and redesigned by Your loving hand so that we never imagine anyone as needing to be discarded or thrown away. Help us to always look for new opportunities to be used in the best possible ways to share Your story with those closest to us.

You made us, and we give You the glory for doing so. Shape us when we need new ideas and new direction or bigger hearts. Mold us to be more like You, serving as examples of all that You are so that others will desire to draw closer to You and be re-formed in Your love.

Amen.

Tattoos

Put me like a seal on your heart, like a seal on your arm.
SONG OF SOLOMON 8:6 NCV

Father God,

In biblical times, the king's seal was an important thing. It showed that the king had authority over people and places and everything in his domain. In our own times, when we put a seal on a document, it means that we see it as legally binding and as something that denotes agreement or perhaps achievement. A seal then indicates that something very significant has happened.

You carry each of us as a seal on Your heart, like a tattoo on Your arm. That means we are a visible part of You and that we are never far from Your thoughts and Your love. You have deemed us to be worthy of You, and that is a gift of Your grace. Help us to identify ourselves with You so that when You look at the seal with our name on it, You feel pleased and are glad to share our stories with others. Help us strive to be worthy of the binding agreement that stands between us that was sealed by our Lord Jesus on the cross.

All that we are depends on You being steadfast, never changing, never giving up on us. We are sealed together in a bond of love that nothing can separate. Thank You for loving us beyond our ability to even understand. Your devotion to us and our devotion to You is everything.

Amen.

Expressions of Love

· ·

*Though I speak with the tongues of men and of angels, but have
not love, I have become sounding brass or a clanging cymbal.*

1 Corinthians 13:1 nkjv

Dear Lord,

We express love in a lot of ways these days. Sometimes we do it in little ways by sending greeting cards, making phone calls, or even sending sweet text messages. We share our hearts quickly and move on to the business of the day. It's all good, but sometimes I long for the expressions of love that came before technology. I yearn for the love notes that were written by hand, or the flowers that come unexpectedly. I even imagine that the lovers in the Song of Solomon were better off, more willing to share their hearts' desires than most of us might be since they expressed their deep love face-to-face.

Of course, love needs to be expressed well beyond the circles of romance. It needs to be shared with our children and our friends. It needs to be felt by those we work with and those who share time with us in various activities no matter where we are. Love needs to speak kindly and with intention no matter when it raises its voice. Love needs to be shared with everything our hearts can give.

Lord, help us to express love in the authentic ways that reveal the truth we carry in our hearts for each other. Grant that we would never simply be clanging cymbals or e-mail gurus. Help us to see each person in our lives as worthy of our love because You have already deemed them to be worthy of Your love.

Amen.

Counting Your Sheep

He said to him the third time, "Simon, son of Jonah, do you love Me?" Peter was grieved because He said to him the third time, "Do you love Me?" And he said to Him, "Lord, You know all things; You know that I love You." Jesus said to him, "Feed My sheep."

JOHN 21:17 NKJV

Father in heaven,

I'm not always sure what it means to "feed Your sheep." I realize that You have called us not only to follow You but also to guide others to the path so that they can follow You as well. I pray that You would help me recognize those people in my life who are searching for You. Help me to be willing to share what I have to feed them with Your Word and with Your promises of hope and love.

The apostle Peter had the opportunity to share conversation and daily walks with You, and yet You still questioned his willingness to help bring others to You. I know that in some ways, I have the same opportunities. You know me and we have spent many hours together, so You know all that I can do. I pray that out of love for You, I would be willing to be a good shepherd, willing to tend those who may not yet know You.

Bless all those who work for Your kingdom today. Help them to show the love they hold for You to everyone they encounter. Bless the work of their hands, and inspire their hearts to do all that they can to feed Your sheep. Help me also to commit my work, my life, and my heart to You in every way.

Amen.

Stretch and Bend

"If you would prepare your heart, and stretch out your hands toward Him. . .your life would be brighter than noonday. Though you were dark, you would be like the morning."

JOB 11:13, 17 NKJV

Dear God,

It's amazing that we can live in a world that is so fast-paced and tech savvy. We can figure out how to send people into space and how to cure diseases, but we still can't figure out how to stretch our hearts so that we can draw closer to You. We can't figure out how to bend in ways that allow each person the space and the opportunity they need to develop in ways for which they were uniquely designed. We take a step ahead and then fall miserably behind.

Help us to prepare our hearts so that we can stretch our minds and spirits and grasp Your hand each day. Help us to reach up when we feel anxious and to stand firm when we face moments of uncertainty. Give us the steadfast desire to grow into the people You meant for us to be.

I pray that more people around the world would crave a heart like Yours and that they would seek ways to make life easier for at least one other person. I ask that You give me a deeper connection to Your Spirit so that I would recognize ways that I can stretch and bend to help blot out the darkness and offer those around me a dose of the noonday sun. Bless the lives of Your children today, and stretch their hearts to meet with Yours.

Amen.

Silly Me

. . . .

*Then David said to God, "I have sinned greatly
by what I have done! Now, I beg you to forgive me,
your servant, because I have been very foolish."*

1 Chronicles 21:8 NCV

Lord God,

I come before You blushing. I'm embarrassed to confess how foolish I've been. I've done things that I know in my heart are wrong, and I ask Your forgiveness. Sometimes I don't even understand why I do the things that I know will grieve my spirit and Yours. I pray You will forgive me once again and help me as I strive to do better.

I pray, too, for those around me who may also do foolish things. We might come before You and give You the sad excuse that we're only human. The problem with that excuse is that You designed us and You know we're capable of much better things. When we stand at a crossroads, tempted by those things that are not right in Your eyes, and most likely not even right in our own eyes, then guard us. Protect us against our own poor choices. Strengthen our resolve to seek Your face before we choose to do anything. Help us to come to You first.

Thank You for knowing us better than we know ourselves and for Your steadfast and loving grace and mercy. None of us could stand before You without Your provision for our foolishness, redeemed in Christ our Savior. Thank You for giving us continual chances to try again.

Amen.

The Good Side of a Broken Heart

*The sacrifice God wants is a broken spirit. God, you will
not reject a heart that is broken and sorry for sin.*

<small>Psalm 51:17 NCV</small>

Dear Lord,

As I strive to live a more heart-shaped life, I'm learning that
it often brings me to my knees, reminding me of the many times I
made the poorest choices and took the wrong road. Those memories grieve me, and even though I've asked forgiveness for them
in days past, they still sadden my spirit whenever I think of them.

I recognize that we can't go back and erase the wrongs, the
crazy times when we simply were not walking closely with You. We
can't even forgive ourselves as much as we wish we could, and so
the pain of those memories lives on.

You have said that once You've forgiven us that You don't
remember our sins anymore. That's an amazing thought and one
that gives me hope. Only You can see what motivates the hearts
of Your children, and only You know when to release us from the
shame of our past wrongs.

I pray today for all of us who have contrite and broken hearts,
weary with the sadness created at our own hands. Help us to
choose the right road from now on, the one that leads us safely
home to You.

Amen.

Lost and Found

*God is truly good to Israel, to those who have pure hearts.
But I had almost stopped believing; I had almost lost
my faith because I was jealous of proud people.*

PSALM 73:1–3 NCV

Father in heaven,

This passage from the Psalms pulls at my spirit and grieves my heart when I consider that I, too, have been jealous of those who don't struggle the way I do. It seems like those who don't respect or acknowledge You are doing far better in the world than I am. They don't worry about tomorrow because their storehouses are full.

Meanwhile, I pray to You for protection and provision and help in nearly every area of my life, but I still come up short. I have no sense of security or even provision beyond today. I come and sit at Your feet every day and share my worries and my hopes.

Ah! There it is! There is the gift! The people that I feel jealous about, the ones who don't seem to have a care in the world, are living in utter poverty! They have lost their way. They have no relationship with You!

Lord, forgive me when I overlook the most amazing part of my life here on earth. I understand more clearly than ever that I am not lost, but I have been found in You. Thank You for spending each new day with me.

Amen.

A Hopeful Heart

But the LORD looks after those who fear him,
those who put their hope in his love.
PSALM 33:18 NCV

Father in heaven,

I am surrounded by people who are not sure if You are there for them. They don't know if they can put their hope in You because the things they've hoped and prayed for in the past have not come to fruition. My heart goes out to them because I understand how that feels and how discouraging it is.

I don't claim to understand the experiences You've shared with me that show me how close You are when I am in a crisis. You show up so often, and You've done so much for me, I'm truly humbled. I count my blessings every day, and I'm grateful for the hope I feel and the love we share.

Help me to be a light, a new source of joy and hope for others. Help me to remind those who suffer that You do know their hearts and the needs of their lives. I pray to be a messenger of hope in any way that I can.

Shape our hearts and minds so that we look to You, not only when we're in need of Your help, but simply because we're in need of You. Draw near to us, and grant us the joy of Your presence. I ask this in the name of Jesus.

Amen.

You Were Adopted!

*God decided in advance to adopt us into his own family by
bringing us to himself through Jesus Christ. This is what he wanted
to do, and it gave him great pleasure. So we praise God for the
glorious grace he has poured out on us who belong to his dear Son.*

Ephesians 1:5–6 nlt

Dear God,

Some may not realize that they were adopted. They came into
the world, and You already knew who they were. You stamped
them with Your seal of approval, and You smiled at the work of
Your hands. Oh, they may have lived with an earthly family, but
right from the start they had a heavenly origin. They were given
glorious grace because of Your dear Son.

Talk about awesome planning! You knew each of us were
coming, and You opened a door for us to come back home when
our trip was done. It delighted You to do it just that way, and so
our adoption stands forever. Our heavenly Father is our guardian
and our Savior.

Today is a great day to praise You, Lord, for meeting each
of us at the door of life with a return ticket. I thank You that You
knew exactly the way our hearts needed to be molded to fit into
Your hand and to recognize the part You play in each life. I thank
You that You know all of us so intimately and well. I praise You for
giving us the greatest love we could ever have and for adopting
us as Your children. I praise You and love You with all my heart!

Amen.

The Respect in Your Heart

. . . .

But respect Christ as the holy Lord in your hearts. Always be ready to answer everyone who asks you to explain about the hope you have, but answer in a gentle way and with respect.

1 PETER 3:15–16 NCV

Dear Lord,

Your presence in my life is such an incredible honor, such a gift to my heart, that I offer You praise and respect and love with every breath. I know what You have done to sustain my life and to give me the blessing of hope and a future.

Today I pray for the people who need You but are not sure how to find You. I pray for those who want to know more about You, and I ask that all of us who try to share our faith would do it in ways that honor Your name. We sometimes forget that we were once outsiders, that once we, too, were full of questions and on a path of discovery.

Give us wisdom when we meet someone who is just beginning to sense that You are real. Help us to guide them toward You with gentleness and humility. Help us to see them as You do and embrace the opportunity to encourage others on the path.

Thank You for giving all of us a chance to come back to You when this life is finished. Thank You for loving and respecting us in the things we do. May Your hope be the center of the joy we carry in our hearts all through the day.

Amen.

Speak Kindness

*"My words come from an honest heart,
and I am sincere in saying what I know."*

JOB 33:3 NCV

Dear God,

When I think about all that Job went through—losing his family and his lands and cattle and then suffering physical ailments and the advice of his friends that seemed anything but helpful—I can imagine how he must have felt that he had no more to lose. There was no need for pretense or trying to sway those around him to his view of things. There wasn't really anything left to fight for, except one thing. . .his belief in You. He believed You were still there and in control. In other words, he lived out the idea that You were God and he was not. He could afford to have an honest heart.

I pray to have an honest heart. I pray to be a person who speaks the things I believe and who listens with compassion. I pray to surrender to Your voice no matter what my circumstances may be. I pray to be devoted to You in all things and in all ways.

It's not easy to be truly honest with You, with others, or even with myself, and so I recognize why You were pleased with Job's faith and devotion and why You restored to him everything that he had lost. Help me to trust You completely and to come to You with an honest and contrite heart. Help me to surrender all that I am and all that I hope yet to be to Your tender care.

Amen.

Living Wholeheartedly

In all that he did in the service of the Temple of God and in his efforts to follow God's laws and commands, Hezekiah sought his God wholeheartedly. As a result, he was very successful.

2 CHRONICLES 31:21 NLT

Dear Lord,

C. S. Lewis once said, "It is not your business to succeed, but to do right; when you have done so, the rest lies with God." This quote seems to describe the attitude of King Hezekiah very well. He did all he could in Your service and tried to follow Your commands with his whole heart. In doing so, he was blessed with success.

Lord, I pray for all of us who are achievers. We set a course and go after it, and we hope it means that one day we'll reach our goal. We hope that working hard and doing a good job will get us where we need to go. That all sounds good, but there can be no measure of success without You.

Help us to seek Your guidance and listen for Your voice concerning the work we do, the things we say, and the way we conduct our lives. Help us to seek after You for all things with our whole heart. Teach us to understand the things we can do that will give You pleasure and show You our heartfelt intention. Help us to desire to do everything Your way.

The world defines success by titles and wealth. You define success by our devotion to You. I pray to be steadfast in my faith and to give You my whole heart in love.

Amen.

Those Heart-Shaped Words

"The mouth speaks the things that are in the heart."
MATTHEW 12:34 NCV

Dear Lord,

Today I want to begin by offering You thanks and praise for all You've done in my life. You've stuck with me through my struggles, and You've raised me up when I was lost. You've encouraged me when my heart was troubled, and You've renewed my spirit when the world looked gloomy. You make a difference in my life every day, and I want to give You the praise and the glory for always being with me.

Help me to live a heart-shaped life so that others, too, might recognize how You show up when we are uncertain and how You keep us safely in the palm of Your hand when we are afraid. Help me in any way that I can to show that my life is guided by Your light and that my heart is open to Your call.

I know that many others have served as examples in my life and have helped me to see You more clearly. We need You, and we need each other. I pray for all of us who seek You with our whole heart. I pray that You would let Your face shine on us and grant us favor to do Your work and to share Your love. Thank You, Father, for the awesome things You do each day.

Amen.

The Cavalry or Calvary

. . . .

They called to you for help and were rescued.
They trusted you and were not disappointed.

PSALM 22:5 NCV

Father in heaven,

When I grew up watching old television westerns, I remember that at the bleakest moments a trumpet would sound and the cavalry would come. The people would be rescued, and all would be well. I confess that there are times when I think of You as the cavalry, praying for You to rescue me before some crisis gets out of hand or problems become too much to bear.

In a state of fear and panic, the cavalry seems like the right choice to make. Of course, at that point I'm open to nearly any superhero that might decide to swoop in and save the day. I know that there are times when You do come in and save Your people quickly, even unexpectedly. I realize, though, that the biggest rescue effort for any of us is the one You already made on Calvary. You gave us a hero in the form of Jesus Christ to rescue us all from sin and raise us up to live with You in heaven. That's a rescue effort that can never disappoint us.

I pray today for every person who needs Your help in big ways or small ways. I pray for those who are hanging on and just hoping the cavalry will show up. Help me to show up when someone needs me, and thank You for rescuing my heart and shaping my life.

Amen.

A Courageous Heart

*"Be strong and courageous;
do not be afraid or lose heart!"*
1 CHRONICLES 22:13 NLT

Dear God,

Sometimes I rise in the morning, full of joy and anticipation, ready to do the work You've called me to do with a heart full of gratitude. I love that feeling, and it is a great way to start the day.

The trouble is that problems seem to get up at the crack of dawn. They are ready to jump on every happy thought and are anxious to destroy the good intentions of my heart. Problems simply don't go away. Oftentimes they have been so persistent that I have prayed and prayed about them many times. I've really tried hard to be strong and courageous.

I pray for everyone who needs answers and direction, that You would intervene and strengthen each step they take so that they are never inclined to lose heart. I pray for the people I love and ask You to bless them with mercy and grace and more strength to get through any issues that arise in their lives.

Help all of us to meet a new day with courage and a grateful heart, ready to laugh and love and serve You in every possible way. Thank You for being our strength and our guide.

Amen.

Musings and Missions

His heart was devoted to the ways of the LORD.
2 CHRONICLES 17:6 NIV

Dear Lord,

Each day, I begin again. You offer me a new day and a fresh start, and all I have to do is surrender to You, give You praise and devotion, and everything feels better. Oh, it doesn't always mean the day is fulfilling or the news is good that comes through to my heart and mind from the outside world, but it does mean that I know You're there with me, and it makes all the difference.

The thing that surprises me, though, is that even when I know the difference it makes to start my day with You and walk with You each place I go, I still don't always do it. In my musings about why, I give myself a lot of reasons, more likely excuses, for not sharing my devotion for You more fully. I pray now that all of us who truly seek You with our whole heart will find You and that we will be devoted to You in every way. Forgive us when we make excuses to go on alone, taking on the world and the day as if we had an ounce of control over it. Forgive us for simply ignoring You, the one we love so much.

Help us to rise and shine, and make it our mission to walk and talk and be with You from the early morning sunshine to the evening rise of the moon. Help us to shine Your light because our hearts are so full of You that we can do nothing else. Thank You for loving us with reckless abandon.

Amen.

Then Sings My Soul

Sing to the LORD a new song; sing to the LORD, all the earth.
Sing to the LORD, praise his name; proclaim his salvation
day after day. Declare his glory among the nations,
his marvelous deeds among all peoples.

PSALM 96:1–3 NIV

Dear heavenly Father,

The most amazing thing happens to my spirit anytime I simply stop everything else I might be doing and devote my whole heart and mind and soul to singing Your praises. I love the feeling that fills my heart when I just let my love for You float up to the heavens. I may not know what those times mean to You, but I can say with every breath that I am transformed from the inside out each time I do it. I wonder what it is that makes me hold back so often.

Thank You for this precious gift. When I make more room for You, I know I have more of You to share with others. You strengthen and renew me and give my soul a chance to dance and sing for You. I love to talk about You, and I want to tell everyone I know of the beautiful things You have done for my life. You have turned me around so many times.

Help me to praise Your name in the car, at home, in the shower, or anyplace I am that gives me a chance to sing Your praises. I give You thanks and glory and honor with all my heart.

Amen.

Tell What God Has Done

Come and hear, all you who fear God;
let me tell you what he has done for me.

PSALM 66:16 NIV

Lord God,

We all like stories. I remember when I first started hearing stories about You. I didn't know exactly who You were, but somehow my heart started trusting You were there as soon as we were introduced. As I continued to grow up and began to read about You for myself and to seek Your help for my life through prayer, You showed me more of Yourself. You let me feel Your presence and get to know You, and that has made all the difference. I tell people stories about You because I have experienced Your love and Your mercy and Your grace and forgiveness. You have welcomed me into Your arms.

Help us to keep sharing the stories we have been given by You. Help us to boldly exclaim Your amazing deeds and the continual ways You show up in our lives. When we tell stories about You, we never know who is listening. We never know just what Your Holy Spirit will do with those stories to shape the hearts of others. Remind us of stories we should share wherever we are. Help us to strengthen and encourage others by our witness. The best part of telling stories about You is that they work to strengthen and renew us all over again.

I praise and thank You today for all You do to make Your presence known and to give me many stories to share with those around me.

Amen.

An Honest Heart

· ·

"I know, my God, that you test people's hearts. You are
happy when people do what is right. I was happy to give
all these things, and I gave with an honest heart."
1 CHRONICLES 29:17 NCV

Dear Lord,

You have been teaching me about honesty my whole life. Sometimes the lesson came from observing others, discovering that the truth was not in them. Sometimes You taught me with temptations, and once I yielded to those temptations, You showed me the ways I willingly deceived myself.

I'd like to think that when You look into my heart today, when You test my motivations, You would find an honest heart. I hope and pray You will guide me always to do things for others with a real desire to help them, whether I do so with words or encouragement, with financial help, or simply by being willing to listen to their needs.

One thing I know for sure: I can only truly be happy when I am honest with You. I pray for everyone who seeks to have a heart motivated by truth and love, ready to give as You have taught us to give, ready to be open to Your guidance and Your voice. Help all of us to do the things that please You anywhere we might be so that we never deceive ourselves or others. Thank You for molding me and shaping my heart to Your glory.

Amen.

Grow Power

. . . .

I planted, Apollos watered, but God gave the increase.

1 CORINTHIANS 3:6 NKJV

Dear God,

When You meet each one of us, You start by simply planting a seed. It may be a nudge of our spirits as we hear a sermon or a pull on our heartstrings as a friend shares her faith. It may be that we have a grandmother who prays, and subtly, without any intention on our own part, our hearts begin to see You. At first, we look for You everywhere with a kind of hungry appetite to know everything we can know as quickly as possible. We want to catch up with everyone else who seems to understand You better than we do.

Then for some reason, we let life get in the way or we become teenagers or young adults, and we think we don't really need You anymore. We're enjoying the idea that we have some independence and we can think for ourselves. It feels good, and it seems like something You want for us, too. The problem is that in that process, many of us simply slip away.

But You don't leave us there. You send someone else into our lives, someone who can take us a step further, who can remind us of what we already know and then excite us all over again to keep walking with You, to keep seeking You. It's such a glorious thing because over our lifetime, we can see Your hand at work, Your desire to help us become Your family and to see You as our friend. Thank You for providing the growing power, because faith is a gift from You, and You alone plant the initial seed deep within our hearts. Help us grow stronger in You each day.

Amen.

It's a Scary World

God, examine me and know my heart;
test me and know my anxious thoughts.

PSALM 139:23 NCV

Creator God,

It's hard to understand that part of me that even imagines I can somehow hide out from You. Maybe it's some link to our ancestors back in the garden who simply wanted to run and hide when they had done something they knew was wrong. Maybe we just don't get that You know us better than we know ourselves.

What I've learned about You, though, is that no matter how long I choose to carry around my worries, my sins, or my actions that I know are not up to Your standards, it's all foolish of me. It's foolish because the quicker I come back to You and seek Your forgiveness, the sooner I can get on with those things that keep us both feeling much better.

Today I ask You to examine my heart and test my thoughts. Help me to surrender every worry and every fleeting idea that will not serve You. Give me the strength and the desire to do greater things for the sake of Your kingdom than I have been willing to do before.

It's a scary world, and sometimes I want to hide from those crazy people out there. Like Jonah, I don't want to go to Nineveh; and yet, I know You need me to be bold and step out in faith each day of the year. Hold me close to You and guard my heart, because I'll go where You want me to go.

Amen.

Trying to Obey Again

With all my heart I try to obey you.
Don't let me break your commands.
PSALM 119:10 NCV

Dear Lord,

Perhaps part of having an honest heart is to be truly motivated to obey Your commands. It seems easy enough to imagine that I wouldn't get so off track that I would steal or murder or commit some other violent crime. The problem is that no matter which commandment I look at, there's a stumbling block. I can honor my parents; but if I don't visit them or call them or do things to make life better for them, I do not honor them very well. I may not murder, commit adultery, or steal; but if I get angry at someone who has done me wrong or imagine even for a moment what it would be like to be with someone other than my spouse, I've fallen again. I don't need to really steal something; if I steal someone's hope or add to their depression, I'm a thief. If I wish too much for a better house or a better car or something that my neighbor has that I don't, I fail again.

What I understand, Lord, is that there is only one way to truly obey these commands, and that is with Your help. On my own, I fail miserably. With You, I am guided into making better choices. Thank You for always being there to help me do the right thing. Thank You for giving me the freedom to choose to obey You and for giving me the strength to do so.

Give me a heart that is willing and ready and able to be obedient to You in all things. Thank You for loving me so much.

Amen.

Sold Out for Jesus!

*Paul and Timothy, both of us committed servants of
Christ Jesus, write this letter to all the followers of Jesus.*
PHILIPPIANS 1:1 MSG

Dear Lord,

I remember when I first gave You my heart. I was practically glowing with love and light and a desire to tell the whole world about You. It was an indescribable feeling and felt like a gift directly given from You to me.

Over the years, I've let the embers die down a bit, maybe because that's just what happens in new love. Now, though, I realize my commitment is actually stronger than ever. Now I know You like I never did before. You've been with me through a lot of ups and downs and given me strength when I had none of my own. You've helped me make choices I couldn't make alone, and You've protected my heart and quieted my spirit. Nothing about my life would be the same without You. I may have bought into You back then, but I'm sold out for You now.

Thank You for helping to keep the bonds between us strong. You've done that by being faithful to me when my heart was troubled, by calming me when a crisis came up, and by hearing the prayers of my heart and mind when my soul was in anguish. Thank You for keeping Your side of the commitment we made to each other. I pray that You will be sold out on me, too. I praise Your name!

Amen.

What Is My Value?

*So I gave up in despair, questioning
the value of all my hard work in this world.*

ECCLESIASTES 2:20 NLT

Dear Lord,

Sometimes despite all my efforts, life falls apart. My work doesn't seem to go anywhere. My finances fall through the floor. No matter how hard I try, I can't seem to make a difference. Even though I bring my concerns to You each day and pray for guidance and direction, I can't feel Your presence, much less Your answers.

Despair is not easy for me. I spend most of my time looking for the positive side of life, looking for the possible when others can't see it. Since I do that anyway and find it usually serves me well, it's even more difficult to have times when everything grinds to a halt. I feel lost, like I made a wrong turn and ended up on some other planet.

I pray today for Your help when those times happen, not just for me but for everyone who suffers from misery, worry, and despair. I pray that You would come and make Yourself known, filling our hearts with hope so that we can feel You are near. What we do for a living only has value in how much it serves You. I ask that You give each of us a sense that all is well in spite of how it feels or appears. Thank You for Your steadfast love and faithfulness.

Amen.

A Leap of Faith

So faith comes from hearing the Good News, and people hear the Good News when someone tells them about Christ.

ROMANS 10:17 NCV

Father in heaven,

I pray today to be willing to share the good news and tell others about Jesus Christ. Forgive me when I am reluctant to spread the word about You and to shine a light on all that You have done for me. Help me to build my own faith and the faith of those around me by sharing the stories You've placed on my heart.

I know that most of us relate to stories. We love the medical dramas and the crime dramas on TV. We enjoy reality shows so we can discover more about the ways others choose to live. We identify with each other more clearly by the stories we share.

As I go about my business today, help me to be a storyteller. Help me to smile and laugh and lend a hand and simply be present for someone who may understand Your story better by the things I do. We all need to grow in faith and in awareness of You, Lord, and so I pray to be an ambassador of Your love and Your truth wherever I am. Help me to simply share the good news!

Open our eyes to opportunities to tell stories, and open our ears to listen for Your voice.

Amen.

Twists and Turns

*For the LORD is God, and he created the heavens
and earth and put everything in place. He made the
world to be lived in, not to be a place of empty chaos.
"I am the LORD," he says, "and there is no other."*

ISAIAH 45:18 NLT

Father of all,

I am reminded today that when You first created the heavens and the earth, forming them from chaos, You created everything to be good. Once You completed Your task and saw that Your new world was ready for human beings to inhabit it, You made it so. The thing that gives my heart joy is knowing that Your first thought was to place people in a garden, a place of peace and harmony, beauty and sustainable life. It was Your plan that we should not have lives of great anxiety, layered by twists and turns in directions we simply can't understand. It was intended for us to trust You and to live with You side by side.

That picture is so beautiful, and though the world today is very far from the mark You once set, there are glimpses of it that remain. We can feel Your presence in our lives when we draw near to You and seek Your face. We can live in Your protection and warmth, giving You thanks for our daily bread and laying our cares at Your feet. Lord, remind us to draw close to You and to do all we can to bring peace and harmony to our lives. Give us grace and kind words to share with our friends and neighbors and families. Help us to be the people You created us to be even now. Thank You for shaping our lives to be more like Yours.

Amen.

Keeping Up with the Neighbors

*We who are strong ought to bear with the failings of the
weak and not to please ourselves. Each of us should
please our neighbors for their good, to build them up.*

Romans 15:1–2 NIV

Dear God,

In our culture, we're often tempted to look at what the neighbors have that we don't. They have the best lawn or the nicest car on the block. They have that great yard or the bay windows with lots of flowers. Somehow the house we live in doesn't seem to compare. We imagine that we simply can't keep up.

If we allow You to enter our hearts and shape our lives though, Lord, we discover that maybe the neighbors wonder if they can keep up with us. Maybe they long to know You better or to serve You in ways that please You. Maybe they have a great desire to embrace Your Holy Spirit or get to know You through the Word, and they know that we strive to do those things at our house more than they do at theirs.

I pray today that You would give me a greater desire to keep up with the neighbors. Help me to keep a word of encouragement and a deed of kindness ready whenever they beckon me. Help me to pray for them and to help them in any way I can to know more about You. Help me to be a neighbor who puts those around me ahead of myself and seeks their good in every possible way.

Yes, Lord, help me to keep up with my neighbors in ways that please You; encourage them, and let the light of Your love shine through. Bless our whole neighborhood today.

Amen.

A Little More Joy

....

Clap your hands, all you nations;
shout to God with cries of joy.
PSALM 47:1 NIV

Dear Lord,

You probably are more used to all the complaining and the crying Your children do than You are used to hearing us shout to You in words of thanksgiving and great joy. When I think about that, it gives me pause and makes my spirit a little sad. After all, we are nothing without You. We are simply dust.

It seems like the whole planet is somehow suffering from a bit of global depression. We all live with anxiety and wonder what we will face the next day that we barely dealt with today. We have given our power away to the world, letting it defeat us and bring us down. We must make Your heart sad when we do this.

Help all of us to trust in You and the plans that You have for our good. Help us to believe like we have never believed before that You can do all things and that nothing is impossible for You. Then, once we have that belief solidly in our hearts and minds, let us rejoice in You and clap our hands and sing Your praises.

We are Your children, safe in Your hands, and we thank You and praise You and surrender our apathy and depression, raising our hearts and minds instead toward You with great love.

Amen.

I Am Grateful

*Praise the LORD! I will thank the LORD with
all my heart in the meeting of his good people.*

PSALM 111:1 NCV

Lord God,

Cicero once wrote, "A thankful heart is not only the greatest virtue, but the parent of all other virtues."

It seems odd that human beings do not begin each day bowed low to You in gratitude for Your tender mercies and abounding grace. You provide so much for us, and yet we seldom give You the praise and glory. I pray that You would open my heart right now to be filled with this virtue of gratitude. If I were to list all that You have done to sustain my well-being, I suspect I could not count the details, nor even remember every kindness You have extended to me.

Even so, Lord, I recognize that I had no hand in the creation of the planet, or in the parents who bore me, or in the circumstances of my life, for these things were ordained by You long before I was born. I am eternally grateful to You.

Help me to live in humble gratitude for the protection and provision and endless love and mercy You have given me. Help me to be grateful for what I have, counting each thing as a miracle in itself. I praise and thank You with a heart full of love.

Amen.

You Know My Heart

· ·

He made their hearts and
understands everything they do.
PSALM 33:15 NCV

Father in heaven,

It seems that You may know me far better than I know myself. At times, I am not even certain of the actions I've taken or the choices I've made. I know that most of the time my intentions are good, but for some reason, good does not come out of me at every opportunity. I do those things that I regret and then look back and question my actions.

Thank You for giving me a heart that reflects on my actions and seeks to determine those things that were good and that were done in the spirit of love and kindness. Thank You for helping me to discover more of what motivates me so that I can work on those things that don't please either of us and do more of the things that are good.

Help me understand the best ways to make my days worthwhile and my work more fulfilling. I pray that my heart will be filled with Your Spirit and guided by Your love. When I don't understand myself or the actions of others, remind me that You are busy molding and shaping each circumstance to give us all we need to make good choices. Give us hearts that hold You close each day so that we can know You better all the time.

Amen.

Blessings and Curses

This day I call the heavens and the earth as witnesses against you that I have set before you life and death, blessings and curses. Now choose life, so that you and your children may live and that you may love the LORD your God, listen to his voice, and hold fast to him.

DEUTERONOMY 30:19–20 NIV

Dear God,

Help me each day as I continue to learn what it means to "choose" You. Help me to recognize that when I made the choice to accept Jesus into my heart, it was meant to be not only a choice but a means of transforming my life. Over the years, You have strengthened my understanding of who You are and what it means to be faithful to Jesus. You have guided my steps and listened to my prayers. You have even changed some of my bad habits into healthy ones.

I've come to understand that some of the things that I look at as "curses" in my life are ones that I brought on myself. I chose to invite trouble in simply because I wasn't willing to seek Your guidance or ask for Your blessing and direction. I know that I cannot have a divided heart and that the best thing I can do is to listen for Your voice and hold fast to Your Spirit. It's not easy in my daily life to always say and do the right thing, the godly thing.

Please help all of us who seek Your blessings to draw closer to You. Give us mercy and forgiveness when we do things that might invite a negative response to who we are and what we do. Show us the way to live in truth and light and joy.

Amen.

Calling On You Again, Lord

. . . .

I prayed to you with all my heart.
Have mercy on me as you have promised.
PSALM 119:58 NCV

Dear God,

It's me again, calling on Your name and praying for Your for-giveness and mercy. It seems that I have not learned as much as I pretend I have about self-control or being kind. I imagine that I'm quite capable of those things, and I genuinely believe I make a great effort in that direction, but my failings are all too apparent. How disappointed You must be!

This time, though, I don't come to You with promises that I will only break at the next opportunity. I don't come to You with a sense that I simply have learned this lesson so well that it can never happen again. I don't even come to You as someone who actually knows why I do the crazy things I do.

I come to You only as a person with a contrite heart. I know that I blew it and that the only way to feel better is to fall on my knees and lay everything at Your feet. Show me how to stay strong and how to trust myself to do the right things. Show me Your mercy and Your grace as I go forward into the day. Help me not only to treat the people around me with respect and humility and forgiveness but also to do the same things for myself.

I believe that You make a difference in my life. Help me to make a difference in the lives of others.

Amen.

Bless My Family

. . . .

"Please, bless my family. Let it continue
before you always. Lord GOD, you have said so.
With your blessing let my family always be blessed."
2 SAMUEL 7:29 NCV

Heavenly Father,

I pray for families everywhere, all across the earth. I pray for those who seek Your face and need Your provision and protection. I pray for those who are trusting You to show them how to survive in this world. Bless them! Bless every family that looks to You for guidance and love and forgiveness.

Open their eyes to see Your hand at work in the things they do. Open their hearts to receive Your counsel and Your blessings. Shine a light on their hopes and dreams, and open doors for opportunities to prevail that will strengthen them and refresh their spirits.

Take care of the children in each family and keep them safe. Draw each parent and child closer to You, and watch over them as a mother hen protects her little flock. Post a guardian angel at their door to shield them from trouble of any kind. Bless them with good health and with treasured family gatherings. Prepare their tables with nutritious foods and their hearts with laughter and warm conversation. Give them peace.

In all things and in every possible way, Lord, I pray that You would bless the families of Your children each day.

Amen.

Come Back Tomorrow

. . . .

*Whenever you are able, do good to people who need help.
If you have what your neighbor asks for, don't say, "Come back
later. I will give it to you tomorrow." Don't make plans to hurt
your neighbor who lives nearby and trusts you.*

PROVERBS 3:27–29 NCV

Dear Lord,

I pray today for the procrastinators. No matter how efficient we are with getting the house cleaned or getting the work done at the office, we sometimes fall short of getting the work done with our neighbors. It's never quite the right time to stop everything and pay a visit or lend a hand.

This momentary selfishness is something we don't even pay attention to because we believe our personal priorities are really the important aspects of any day. We don't even consider that You may have prompted an exchange with a neighbor, and by neighbor, I don't just mean the people who live near us but anyone who seeks our help.

Expand our ideas about what it means to be a neighbor. Give us more generous hearts, open to the needs of others and willing to help however we can. Sure, there are days when we simply keep on the path we set, but often, we could indeed change our course. We don't have to simply suggest that someone in need "come back tomorrow."

Thank You for those who remind us of our humanity and how good it feels to offer our help. After all, that is how we serve You the best.

Amen.

Clap Your Hands

*Clap your hands, all you nations; shout to
God with cries of joy. For the LORD Most High
is awesome, the great King over all the earth.*

Lord Most High,

Your people around the world celebrate their relationship with You. They love to clap their hands and share their hearts with anyone who will listen. They love to tell what You have done. You are indeed a glorious King, and we are humbled that You love us so much.

I pray today for those who are still sitting on the proverbial fence, wondering if You are real and wanting to know more about who You are. I pray that their eyes will be opened and that Your Spirit will prevail in their lives. I pray for the people who are afraid of You, either afraid they are not worthy of Your love or simply afraid that their sins are too great for You to handle.

Help those of us who know You to share Your stories and tell all that You have done. When we do that, I pray that Your Holy Spirit would fill the room or the space where we speak and touch the hearts of each one who hears the message.

It looks bleak in the world, and it feels like total chaos. It's hard for people to hear You speaking because of the noise that overwhelms their lives each day. Be with us all so we can clearly understand Your direction and continue to celebrate the joy of being part of Your family. Thank You for sustaining us, providing for our needs, and keeping us safe in Your hands.

Amen.

Forever and Ever, Amen!

· ·

My heart is steady, God; my heart is steady.
I will sing and praise you.
PSALM 57:7 NCV

Dear God,

I don't always think about it, but there is something amazing about realizing that my heart is steady, sturdy, stable. That means that I am fixed on You in a way that does not vacillate in any significant way. That idea helps me to understand how powerful it is to know that You have steadfast love for me and Your children throughout the earth. You are steady all the time. You love us all the time. I praise You with every beat of my heart for drawing so close to us.

Lord, there are still a lot of people who do not know You or who have not understood Your steadfast love and faithfulness. I pray for them today so that they may be lifted up to You and held close to You. Open their ears to hear Your name being glorified. Open their eyes to see the works of many who labor out of love and devotion to further Your kingdom. Give them an understanding about the benefits they, too, could enjoy when they lay their burdens at Your feet and steady themselves in Your mighty hand.

Even though we are earthbound, which means we have blinders on when it comes to seeing You as You really are, I pray that You will break through our fears and our doubts and help us to sing Your praise forever and ever!

Amen.

Turning toward the Son

While he was still speaking, a bright cloud covered them,
and a voice from the cloud said, "This is my Son,
whom I love; with him I am well pleased. Listen to him!"

MATTHEW 17:5 NIV

Father in heaven,

No matter what age I happen to be, I still find Your intervention into human welfare and Your desire to draw closer to us amazing. I am in awe of the very fact that You sent Your beloved Son, Jesus, to this earth to save us from ourselves and the sins we commit every day of the week. We are lost without You, and some of us don't even realize how lost we are.

Help us to turn back to You and to lay our troubles down. Help us to cross over the abyss of doubt and to desire nothing more than to know You with truth and certainty and love. Stretch our hearts to make them big enough to receive You in ways we never thought were possible. Forgive us when we seek You only with our minds and leave our hearts far behind.

You are amazing because You make it so simple for us to live in Your love and faithfulness. You gave us a tiny baby, nurtured our understanding of Him, and then caused us to grieve at His death simply because we could see that Your motive for all of it was love—love for Him and love for us. You are an awesome God, and we cannot begin to perceive the depth and height and width of all that You are and all that You would choose to be in our lives. Help us to listen to Your Son and to Your Holy Spirit and to Your voice our whole life through. We praise Your name.

Amen.

Couldn't Live without You!

Lord, my God, I will praise you with all my heart,
and I will honor your name forever.

PSALM 86:12 NCV

O Lord, my God,

I pray today that You would help me to honor You with my whole heart. Help me to desire more of You and less of me and to choose in every possible way to strengthen Your name. You are the God of my heart. You are the love of my life, and I know that there is nothing about my work or my family or the people I love that is essential without You.

Help me to grow and change and become a more consistent prayer warrior. Help me to lay before You the things that concern my heart and stifle my life. Cause me to choose You when temptations arise or when pressures from the outside world threaten me. Make my heart big enough to contain all the love You have for me and all the love You want me to share with others.

When my heart is challenged by doubt, strengthen and renew me so that certainty prevails. I pray for everyone who seeks You in their heart, who hopes in Your guidance and Your steadfast love. I pray for Your light to shine in our hearts in ways that are even beyond our understanding. I pray that we all would honor Your name and choose to listen to Your voice so that we can truly live heart-shaped lives.

Amen.

A Prayer for a Heart-Shaped Life

. . . .

All who call on God in true faith,
earnestly from the heart,
will certainly be heard,
and will receive what they have asked and desired,
although not in the hour or in the measure,
or the very thing which they ask;
yet they will obtain something greater and more glorious
than they had dared to ask.

MARTIN LUTHER

Scripture Index

OLD TESTAMENT